Where the Sun Don't Shine

Where the Sun Don't Shine

Hugh Graham

TORONTO

Exile Editions
2000

This edition is published by Exile Editions Limited, 20 Dale Avenue, Toronto, Ontario, Canada   M4W 1K4

Sales Distribution:
McArthur & Company
c/o Harper Collins
1995 Markham Road
Toronto, ON
M1B 5M8
toll free:
1 800 387 0117
(fax) 1 800 668 5788

Layout and Compostion by *TIM HANNA*
Typeset at *MOONS OF JUPITER, INC.* (Toronto)
Printed by *AGMV MARQUIS*

THE CANADA COUNCIL | LE CONSEIL DI
FOR THE ARTS | DU CANADA
SINCE 1957 | DEPUIS 1957

ONTARIO ARTS
COUNCIL

CONSEIL DES ARTS
DE L'ONTARIO

The publisher wishes to acknowledge the assistance toward publication of the Canada Council and the Ontario Arts Council.

ISBN 1-55096-527-1

A HIGH RIDGE OF PLOUGHED LAND.

Against the sky, a plough and a team of horses idle, unattended.
Black smoke drifts upward from behind the ridge.

Over the ridge and below, a wrecked train lies smouldering and
smoking on twisted railway tracks. Figures move about among the
wreckage.

Through the smoke, several men, farmhands by their appearance,
browse about examining and sifting through the wreckage, litter
and debris — the scattered belongings of passengers — casually,
almost as if they were at an auction.

A farmhand named Isaac, with a chin-beard, picks up a suitcase
from among the litter and good linen shirts tumble out onto the

grass as it falls open. He sorts through it, opens out a good shirt, looks at it, puts it under his arm. A massive, taciturn man, Elmer, joins Isaac. He carries a woman's parasol and wears an undersized bowler hat on his head.

Elmer, Isaac, and three other brothers further along begin to move back into the field and up the low ridge toward the plough and team, carrying clothes, suitcases, a candelabra and other items.

A RESIDENTIAL STREET AT DUSK, TORONTO, THE YEAR 1904.

Gas lights. Heavy with chestnut trees; commodious, comfortable Edwardian houses, windows warmly lit.

THE DAVENPORT HOUSE. THE DINING ROOM AT DUSK.

Mr. Davenport, a wealthy businessman, and Mrs. Davenport, nervous but matronly, are seated at dinner. The room is heavy with dark wood and knick-knacks. Mr. Davenport is reading the newspaper.

MR. DAVENPORT
Hah! There's been another train accident up in Prince Albert County.

MRS. DAVENPORT
That's the third or fourth up there, isn't it?

Mr. Davenport looks sharply down the table.

MR. DAVENPORT
... Where's ah ... whatshis — ah, you know ... ah ...

MRS. DAVENPORT
(tip of her tongue)
... Latimer. Yes, he says he's had a lot of work to do.

MR. DAVENPORT
(hollers)
Latimer!

LATIMER'S ROOM.

Latimer Davenport sits at a desk, his arms folded, head down. He wakens to his father's shouting — unshaven, thin, pallid, cerebral looking, in contrast to his robust parents. His shirt is buttoned to the neck. He straightens and stares at a diary page dated "June 5" with the words "Wakened, went downstairs ... " The rest of the page is blank.

THE DAVENPORT HOUSE. THE DINING ROOM.

Latimer is seated at the table, sleepy, as if it were morning.

MR. DAVENPORT
What have you been doing up there?

Mr. Davenport speaks while still reading his paper.

Latimer
Thinking ...

Mr. Davenport
All that thinking never seems to've got you a day's work.

Mrs. Davenport
Why don't you go out and find yourself a job once and for all.

Latimer
I have a job, mother.

Mrs. Davenport
Since when?

Latimer
About a year. I work in a bank.

Mrs. Davenport looks at her husband, astonished.

Mrs. Davenport
That's where he goes during the day.

Mr. Davenport
Is the pay any good?

Latimer
(pause)
I was fired about a month ago.

Mr. Davenport lowers his paper.

Mr. Davenport
I spent four years prying lint out of the floor-boards in a yarn mill and then I pulled myself up by my bootstraps with huge windfalls in land speculation. And what have you done? Nothing!

LATIMER
That's the past. There's no challenge any more. No risk.

MR. DAVENPORT
Seems bank-telling was a bit of a risk.

MRS. DAVENPORT
Ask about selling insurance.

LATIMER
No, no, mother, I'm talking about free enterprise, parlaying a nickel into a dollar. Like this automobile thing. You don't just make one. You make a thousand. It's called mass-production.

MR. DAVENPORT
... What a stupid idea ...

LATIMER
Or maybe just go somewhere ... Persia ... Mongolia ... the outer reaches of the empire.

MRS. DAVENPORT
You could go down to the regatta.

MR. DAVENPORT
It's been rained out.

MRS. DAVENPORT
It's not til next week.

MR. DAVENPORT
They're not taking any chances.

LATIMER
There you are. In a place like Persia or Mongolia, they would have gone through with the regatta.

Mr. Davenport folds his paper and places it on the table.

Mr. Davenport
No they would not. They don't have regattas in Mongolia.

Latimer
They have lakes, don't they?

Mr. Davenport
No, they don't have lakes!

Things are getting very tense.

Latimer
All right, lawn bowling then.

Mr. Davenport
They don't have lawn bowling either.

Latimer
Fine! In Madagascar!

Mrs. Davenport
You can't lawn bowl for a living.

Davenport is staring at his newspaper.

Mr. Davenport
I'll tell you what you *can* do. You can start paying your own board. There's an advertisement for farm labour.

Mrs. Davenport
Henry, no.

He tears the ad from the paper.

MR. DAVENPORT
F. Rawlinson, Canaan Post Office, Prince Albert County.

MRS. DAVENPORT
Isn't that where they had the train wreck?

LATIMER
Electricity! There's another thing that's going to make money. With a minimum of investment —

MRS. DAVENPORT
The area is depressed and crime-ridden.

MR. DAVENPORT
Adversity builds character, doesn't it?

MRS. DAVENPORT
I really think that depends ...

MR. DAVENPORT
Clipping the hedge isn't going to pay your way in this house, boy.

THE RAWLINSON FARMHOUSE.

A stark and massive farm house dominates dreary fields under a lowering sky. It is unpainted, almost derelict.

THE RAWLINSON FARM HOUSE. THE KITCHEN.

The room is prematurely dark, suggesting perpetual twilight: shadows, dusty varnish. Time arrested. The terrible tick of a clock. The kitchen door opens. Elmira, an incongruously sensual woman of 18 comes in carrying two buckets of milk. It is hard to believe she could have been born there: the only preserve of feminine charm in the house — likely the entire district. Ellen Rawlinson, a big, heavy-set woman is setting the table for breakfast.

Frank Rawlinson lurches in from a corridor; late fifties, lean, cantankerous with a thatch of black hair and a mean, pointed chin-whisker, undershirt and suspenders, carrying broken work boots.

FRANK
Spring is nigh upon us, we've labour to commence! John! Matthew!

Frank lurches to the table and sits down to put his boots on.

FRANK
(hollers upward)
You sonsofbitches, the property's in a state of morbid dereliction!

The kitchen is a cavernous room with windows and doors onto a back veranda. A big dinner table, ten chairs — torn, water-stained floral wallpaper; a pendulum wall-clock; bric-a-brac, framed family photos. On one inside wall, a framed portrait photograph of an old, whiskered family patriarch, Eben Rawlinson.

In a corner, Elmer, the big taciturn man from the train-wreck — a man of menacing calm and deceptive simplicity — shaves in a cracked mirror. He stands in the way of the milk can. Elmira belts him to make him move and begins to pour the milk buckets into the can.

FRANK
We got that hired man coming up tonight. You got a room ready for him?

ELMIRA
We got no spare room.

FRANK
Where we got Granpa?

Ellen, clearing the table, looks at Frank, perplexed.

ELLEN
He's dead.

FRANK
What?

ELLEN
Granpa's dead.

ELMIRA
He's upstairs in the west bedroom.

ELLEN.
He's dead.

FRANK
(winces, perplexed)
What? ... Bah! He's upstairs!

ELLEN
He is not!

ELMIRA
He was upstairs in the winter, west bedroom when I went in to clean.

There is an uneasy silence. Isaac, the eldest brother, comes in from outside. We recognise the chin-beard. He is wiry, with a touch of demonic charm.

FRANK
You seen Granpa?

ISAAC
He's in his room.

FRANK
(to Ellen)
There you are.

Matthew, a younger brother, comes into the kitchen, half asleep in undervest with suspenders hanging.

MATTHEW
He died in the winter, for God's sakes.

FRANK
He's just been sick, that's all.

Matthew pulls up his suspenders and pulls on a jacket.

MATTHEW
Obituary was in the paper.

ISAAC
Well papers cause trouble printing misinformation like that. He's upstairs.

ELLEN
He is deceased.

Thunder crashes directly overhead. Matthew looks toward the ceiling.

MATTHEW
Could be you're both right.

Everyone, struck speechless, looks upward. After a silence, Matthew and Elmer go outside.

ELLEN
(to Elmira)
Go fix up Granpa's room for the hired help. He'll be here by dark.

Isaac glares at Frank.

ISAAC
I thought we weren't having no more hired men here.

Frank goes out abruptly, closing the door.

ELMIRA
I never minded having hired help.

ISAAC
No, you never did mind having the hired help, did you?

ELMIRA
Who in hell do you think you're —

ISAAC
You had the last one.

Ellen disappears into another room.

ISAAC
Look, you don't need them scratching at your door. You got anything that needs saying, you bring it to your brother.

A RAILWAY LINE. OPEN FARM COUNTRY. AFTERNOON.

The contrast is undeniable. It is bright, arcadian, the sky clear and blue. A passenger train tears along, full steam.

A PASSENGER CAR.

Well-heeled city and resort people, vacationers and a few country people. Light suits, summer dresses, parasols, boaters, a lot of wicker. Among them, Latimer Davenport in blazer and white flannels, a boater. He has beside him a suitcase and reads Nietzsche, *Beyond Good and Evil.* He is watched by two farmers, opposite, in musty, patched suits wearing broken hats. One carries a pitchfork.

FARMER 1
I read that one.

FARMER 2
Did you?

Latimer looks up at them.

LATIMER
Excuse me, can you tell me where I get off for Maskinonge Township?

FARMER 1.
Where the sun don't shine.

LATIMER
Sorry?

FARMER 2
What in hell you want to go up
there for?

FARMER 1
He's likely relatives he has to commit to the asylum.

FARMER 2
Don't get off at Horkimer.

FARMER 1
Nor at Gomorrah.

FARMER 2
It don't go up that far. There was a train
wreck. There's a detour.

FARMER 1
Get off at Canaan.

FARMER 2
If the train derails you gone too far.

LATIMER
Perhaps you can tell me how to get out to —

FARMER 2
Rawlinsons?

LATIMER
Yes, how did you know?

The farmers look at each other ominously.

FARMER 1
(mumbles)
That's pert near all there is up in them thar parts one way or t'other.

LATIMER
Sorry?

FARMER 2
He said,
(he enunciates distinctly)
"That's ... pert ... near all there is ... up in them thar ... parts ... one way or ... t'other.

FARMER 1
You take the Scrag Road straight out, past a little place called Syphilis, second line you cross you're in Maskinonge. You can't miss it.

FARMER 2
It's depressing.

FARMER 1
There's a mental asylum on your left. First right'll take you out by the burned-out Paxton place.

FARMER 2.
Second asylum on your right, turn left, ask from there.

THE RAWLINSON HOUSE.

In front of the house, a horse-drawn hearse, and a crowd of forty or fifty people dressed in mourning. Buggies and horses crowded in.

Not a sound, not a word. Everyone is in the same attitude, staring toward the upper storey.

Near the front door, two old men and a woman. They murmur.

OLD MAN 1
He was a litigious sonofabitch.

OLD MAN 2
What does "litigious" mean?

OLD MAN 1
Nobody never got the better of him in law.

AN OLD WOMAN
I hear the money come out of the railroad.

OLD MAN 2
If it did, he never spent a cent of it on this place.

THE RAWLINSON KITCHEN.

A wake in progress. More crowds. Masses of black satin and broadcloth. The table laid with colourless food. On the staircase stand Michael, Elmer and Isaac, deadpan silent. Isaac watches Elmira serving the mourners. Sealey, a lawyer, climbs the stairs. The brothers watch him suspiciously.

SEALEY
Arthur Sealey of Hanlan, Grattan, Holden, Tomlinson, Grady, Caldwell, Teasedale, Hammil, Portly and Gander, barristers and solicitors.

ISAAC
Upstairs.

The upstairs corridor, suffocated with gloom, lined with mourners. Sealey makes his way toward a crack of light at the end.

THE WEST BEDROOM.

By a battered enamel single bed, Ellen stonily wipes away a tear. Frank looks on grimly. Lawyers and bankers with hats, documents, brief cases look on respectfully.

They are paying their respects to Granpa, who lies, bearded, wizened, dirty and ravaged from neglect, fully alive, staring back at them, eyes shifting warily. Sealey edges through.

GRANPA
What do *you* want?

SEALEY
I'm Arthur Sealey, Mr. Rawlinson, of Hanlan, Grattan, Tomlinson —

GRANPA
(*snaps*)
Grady, Caldwell and on and on and on, get on with it.

SEALEY
We're very sorry to hear of your incipient passage over to the other side.

THE KITCHEN.

The empty coffin is brought through the door, borne by morticians.

THE WEST BEDROOM.

Grandpa watches the lawyers and bankers, and his family. Elmira joins them. She seems genuinely sad.

BANKER
We suspect your funds are not collecting any interest in their present state. If these matters were concluded, I think it would be in the best interests of everyone concerned —

SEALEY
— first and foremost yours, sir.

FRANK
(*sneers*)
Don't be ridiculous.

The banker pushes forward a pen and a document.

BANKER
We can read the small print aloud to you if you like.

GRANPA
I have made my own family my executor.

SEALEY
If I could make a recommendation —

GRANPA
(erupts with surprising force)
Shut up you, chiselling hypocritical, Sunday-temperance basement-drinking whoremongering sonofabitch. If this community wants to settle with my estate. If you ... if ... If you ...
(he flags)
You ...

He loses his words, his breath fails, his eyes glaze over and roll upward. Everyone seems to hang on his last word. Ellen turns abruptly.

ELLEN
All right, pick him up, take him down. They can't get the box past the landing.

Suddenly Granpa explodes in laughter. Everyone recoils in horror.

GRANPA
Get out of here and go to hell all of you! I'll go when I damn well feel like it!

The mourners begin to withdraw. Granpa thunders:

GRANPA
Elmira!

THE KITCHEN.

Elmira looks upward as she hears her name bellowed. She smiles slightly, moves toward the stairs.

THE PASSENGER TRAIN. AFTERNOON.

Latimer is now alone. The other seats are empty; the sun is gone. He is looking forlornly out the window. The sky is heavy, the landscape endless, featureless, dreary. Rolling, eaten-down bad pasture to the horizon. But the two farmers still face him, staring at him gloomily. They rise, one picking up a sack, the other a pitchfork.

FARMER 1
Anon.

FARMER 2.
I don't know what to say.

Latimer sees a sign pull into view; it reads, 'Canaan Station'.

THE RAWLINSON HOUSE. AFTERNOON.

From outside, the cracked window to the west bedroom, paintless, siding loose. Dark, rolling clouds above, thunder.

THE RAWLINSON HOUSE. THE UPSTAIRS CORRIDOR.

Elmira moves down toward the west bedroom, nudges the door open, looks in, screams.

CANAAN STATION.

Latimer stands on the platform; endless country, darkness, thunder. The train diminishing.

THE RAWLINSON HOUSE.

Latimer stands in the roadway, staring. The house deserted, the mourners departed. A steady rain falling.

On the front steps, he raises his hand to knock when the door opens and a coffin lurches out, borne by Michael and John Rawlinson. Latimer dodges and they push past without seeing him. He watches them and turns back to the door as Elmer appears, stares at him blankly. Silence except for the hiss of the pouring rain.

LATIMER
Good afternoon, is this Rawlinsons? I'm Latimer Davenport.

Elmer stares at him impassively.

LATIMER
You advertised for a hired hand?

Elmer continues to stare.

LATIMER
Well it was I ... who answered the advertisement.

There is still no response. Latimer looks around and sees an old nag and wagon standing. Michael and John pitch the coffin over the side and it crashes and clatters.

Elmira suddenly appears in the doorway, shoving Elmer aside. She yells in his ear.

ELMIRA
It's the hired help!
(to Latimer)
Come in.

He is instantly struck by her appearance. He steps in, removing his hat.

LATIMER
Ah, thank you

THE RAWLINSON HOUSE. THE UPSTAIRS CORRIDOR.

Elmira, carrying folded sheets leads Latimer with a lighted candle illuminating the shabby passage with stains from leaking and mildew. They pass several closed doors.

ELMIRA
These rooms is closed off. They were dead relatives.

They arrive at the end door, the door to the west bedroom.

ELMIRA
This here is your room.

She opens the door. Pale light falls across his face which freezes. The walls are warped, the wallpaper torn. Dead flies and empty patent medicine bottles litter the floor and window sill. He notices an overturned chair in the middle of the floor and his eyes drift upward to a piece of frayed rope hanging from a hook in the ceiling. In the corner is a bed, the grimy sheets turned back.

Elmira tosses down the clean sheets, sets down the lamp, begins to strip the bed.

ELMIRA
Open the window.

Latimer crosses to the window, gingerly takes the handles, yanks twice. It will not budge. Heavy nails have been towed in, nailing it shut. He is quite nervous now.

LATIMER
It seems to have been nailed closed.

Elmira dumps the sheets, comes over, yanks the window hard and it grinds upward, bending out the nails and crumbling dried paint.

ELMIRA
This was Granpa's room before.

LATIMER
Before what?

She gazes out the window. Her manner is matter-of-fact, a little distant.

ELMIRA
We call this the room with a view, 'cause it overlooks the drowned land yonder.

A train whistle blasts twice in the distance.

ELMIRA
Six o'clock. Maskinonge Central's back on the rails. They had the wreck Thursday.

Latimer is wondering how he might reverse his decision.

ELMIRA
May as well make yourself comfortable.

He shifts reluctantly and sets down his bag, nods, indicating he's ready to unpack.

LATIMER
Well ...
(pause)
There a town near here?

ELMIRA
Just Canaan, we go in once in a while, ain't nothing there.

LATIMER
Just to get supplies, or ... ?

ELMIRA
Sight-seein.

There is an awkward silence. Elmira is staring at him.

ELMIRA
Them's nice clothes, you don't mind my saying.
(she comes close to him)
You remind me a little of Hiram Bradley, that's all.
(she fingers his lapel)
He'd nice Sunday clothes like you got.

Suddenly from downstairs, Frank hollers:

FRANK
Elmira!

ELMIRA
He was a Free Methodist sewing-machine salesman come round here once.

LATIMER
Someone's calling you.

She takes his hand lightly.

ELMIRA
See, he was a gentleman. He wasn't one to be getting drunk and hit people.

Latimer gazes at her.

ELMIRA
He stayed a while and worked for dad ... and we got to be very good friends ... one night in the culvert down by the ninth line ... We made a secret engagement to be married and then one morning he was gone, no good-bye note nor nothin ... What's more, he took the Bible my Grandpa give me.

Latimer squeezes her hand gently, nervously.

LATIMER
Unfortunate.

ELMIRA
Something must have happened to him.

LATIMER
Are you doing anything later?

ELMIRA
I can't. I got to milk.

She pulls her hand away. He looks distastefully around the room and out the window.

LATIMER
... You interested in coming back down to the city? ... I can get you work there.

ELMIRA
I can't.

She kisses him lightly, moves away.

THE FOOT OF THE STAIRS.

Ellen hollers upward:

ELLEN
Elmira!

THE WEST BEDROOM.

Elmira, closer to the door, staring back at him.

ELMIRA
I gotta go.

LATIMER
There's a future in the city.

ELMIRA
Then what are you doing here?

He has no reply. We hear Frank shout from below.

FRANK
Elmira! You still up there!

Elmira turns and abruptly but softly closes the door.

ELMIRA
(*quickly*)
Look, do you have any prospects back in Toronto?
(*pause*)
Seriously.

We hear approaching footsteps.

ELMIRA
Well, you won't here neither. The work's hard and the pay's terrible. So listen good. My Granpa made a windfall fortune out of that railway land yonder and it's here on this property.

LATIMER
(interest piqued)
What, a cash settlement?

ELMIRA
But it ain't where he told the others it was. He told me different. It might take a while to get it, but I'll need your help.

LATIMER
What sort of amount are we talking about?

We hear Frank holler, yet closer.

FRANK
Elmira? Do your chores, god dammit! We got the burial in an hour!

Elmira points to the window.

ELMIRA
You see them dead elm trees yonder? You meet me there afore dark tomorrow night. I'll be milkin'.

She takes his hand and squeezes it, goes out closing the door, leaving him standing.

FAMILY CEMETERY. DUSK.

Adjacent to a small, steep ravine. A sinking family graveyard with alabaster monuments, broken and listing. The old nag and the empty wagon. Mourners are gathered round an open grave at the ravine's edge. Beyond is blasted, open countryside. The monotonous chant of crickets.

MINISTER
Eben loved his family dearly as they loved and cherished him thankful for the gift of life he passed to each and every one of them, and to the township, the gift of prosperity.

The family ill with poverty and suspicion. Frank, Elmer, Ellen, Isaac, Elmira, John and Michael their glances shifting. A few shabby locals behind them.

MINISTER
And may we all be grateful for the vast and beautiful land God laid to the hand of Eben Rawlinson.

The burial from above — the railway tracks in mid-distance, land cropped and lumbered into nothingness. Ellen Rawlinson dabs a false tear with a calculating, shifting glance at the others.

MINISTER
And the heritage of prodigality which lies deep in the soil for which he cared so dearly.

Elmer looking down, his eyes shifting. Ellen, her glance shifting to Frank. Frank and Isaac's glances meeting, evading. Bitter, sidelong looks among Michael, John, Elmira. The boys lower the coffin into the ground on ropes.

A field mouse scampers among the feet of the mourners. Elmer reflexively stamps on it. The monotonous chant of crickets getting louder. Thunder rumbles.

THE RAWLINSON HOUSE. THE WEST BEDROOM. EVENING.

Latimer sits on the bed, looks around the room, haunted, ambivalent. He looks toward the door, at the frayed rope, the overturned chair. Thunder rolls closer.

THE RAWLINSON HOUSE.

The house in stark silhouette against an inky sky. The crickets fade quite suddenly to silence. The weak light of a lantern wells up in a downstairs window. We hear words shouted, but barely audible.

THE WEST BEDROOM.

Latimer, asleep in bed. He stirs, his eyes open slowly. He listens hard, hearing faint voices, shouting, snarling, quarrelling:

ELLEN
What in hell you doing up this time of night!

FRANK
My father's will is gone!

THE KITCHEN. NIGHT.

Frank, monstrous in the lurid glow of the lantern he carries, lurching in, suspenders and trousers pulled on over long johns. A crowbar in his other hand.

FRANK
I'd like to know who the bastard was, was up there!

He gets down and tears up a floorboard near the kitchen wall.

THE WEST BEDROOM. NIGHT.

Latimer in bed, listening. We hear crashing, footsteps, a door slamming downstairs.

MATTHEW
You're keeping everybody up, you fool!

FRANK
You up in the west bedroom this morning?
(Pause)
Answer me, you sonofabitch!

Heavy footsteps, a door slams.

ISAAC
(from elsewhere)
She's a whore, I tell you!

MATTHEW
Who you calling a whore?

MICHAEL
It was her was up there with him!

JOHN
You're a liar.

FRANK
I said, who was the bastard!

Indecipherable snarling and shouting, followed by running footsteps; a door slams followed by two shotgun blasts. Latimer half sits up, remains absolutely still. Then we hear the sudden crash of thunder followed by heavy rain on the roof.

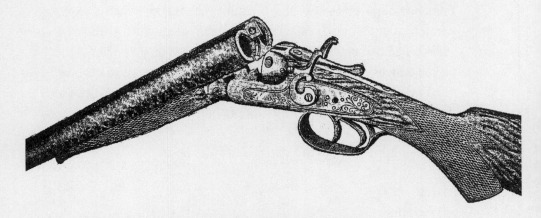

THE FAMILY GRAVEYARD. NIGHT.

The listing monuments in torrential rain. Mud oozes. The entire graveyard shifts. Thunder splits the air; lightning illuminates monuments moving. Cracks open in the ground. The freshly covered grave sinks as the whole embankment collapses, a torrent of mud heaving downward in the deluge — the coffin itself lurching outward as if the ground itself were giving birth — the coffin lid split and then askew, a dead white forearm protruding.

THE RAWLINSON FARM. DAWN.

The house and outbuildings in decrepit silhouette against the dawn sky. We hear a rooster crow.

THE RAWLINSON KITCHEN.

All of the Rawlinsons except for Elmira, gathered at the table. These are the people Latimer will have to live with: a foreign land with foreign people. The ambience is dour, work-worn. Frank and Ellen sit at opposite ends. The Rawlinson men wear worn and patched dark suits — bucolic, threadbare bankers — vests, jackets, watch chains, some unshaven, all of them sunburned, with large, blackened and cracked hands. Elmira's place is next to Ellen's. The two youngest, John and Michael, sit beside Elmer. Opposite sits Isaac and beside him, the scruffy Matthew, who seems to be asleep; next to Matthew an empty seat with an empty bowl.

Latimer appears from the stairs. He smiles hesitantly.

LATIMER
Good morning.

They do not acknowledge him. At length Ellen glances at him, nods brusquely to the empty place. Latimer quietly crosses and sits down. An awkward silence. He looks at his empty bowl, looks up, smiles.

LATIMER
Bit of a storm last night.

An undirected murmur from Isaac, answered by a mumble from John, followed by silence. Latimer looks abruptly down.

LATIMER
Anyway, it's a lovely morning.

ELLEN
No it ain't.

Frank looks at Latimer as if he were out of his mind.

JOHN
It's overcast.

FRANK
(hollers)
Elmer!
(he hollers louder)
El-mer!

Latimer petrified, stares downward.

ELLEN
(to Latimer)
You expect it to be brought to you?

LATIMER
Sorry?

ELLEN
Your breakfast! It's been settin on the stove since five this mornin. You want to be waited on hand and foot?

LATIMER
Sorry, I just help myself or —?

ELLEN
No one else is going to.

A few brothers give out a laugh.

MICHAEL
(repeating, laughing)
No one else is going to.

Latimer rises with his bowl. The outside door opens. He takes a quick and direct look at Elmira as she comes in with a bucket of milk. Her eyes glance past Latimer's. He helps himself to porridge and sits down.

FRANK
(to Latimer, mumbling)
You ever tray in a dell down to nether bottom in cant-hook, ever for nigh on a titch in hell?

LATIMER
I'm sorry, I —

ELMIRA
It's a dialect.

FRANK
I asked you how long it would take you to draw a cord of unsplit elm two chains and a rod out of a creek-bottom using a cant-hook.

Latimer is caught short.

LATIMER
(he fakes it)
A cant — A ... a day, roughly.

FRANK
(hollers)
Elmer! ... He still upstairs asleep?

ELMER
I'm here ... I'm sitting here.

ELLEN
(to Frank)
Not so loud, the lad's hard of hearing.

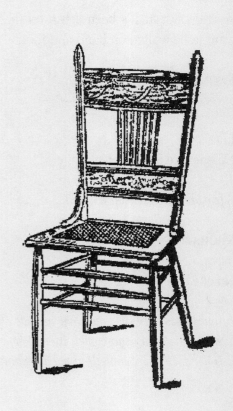

FRANK
It's all right, just pass the cream.

ELMER
It's Tuesday.

ELLEN
Matthew, pass him the cream ... I said pass him the cream. What's got into you?

Matthew, asleep next to Latimer.

ELLEN
(to the others)
What's wrong with *him* now?

ISAAC
Resting likely.

ELLEN
He ain't resting, he's thinking. That's what's wrong with him. I told you people time and again not think but you don't listen.
(shouts)
Matthew!

FRANK
(his mouth full)
He's dead.

ELLEN
(mild alarm)
What?

Isaac looks uneasily at Matthew, shoves him slightly.

ISAAC
Looks all right to me.

Latimer looks uneasily at Matthew next to him. The others scrutinize him.

FRANK
He was dead when I come down this morning.

Latimer, a spoonful of porridge posed before his mouth.

ELLEN
Why didn't you say so?

FRANK
I didn't want an
emotional scene.

ELLEN
Least you could have
done was —

FRANK
We're not Catholics here.

Matthew sinks forward to the table, upsetting a mug of tea. There is a ragged shotgun wound in his back. Latimer replaces the spoon in his bowl.

ELLEN
Well, what happened to him?

ISAAC
Shot, by the looks of it.

LATIMER
Shot?

ISAAC
In the back.

FRANK
Wasn't me.
(he surveys the others)
Now who was it? Own up, this is a serious matter.
(to Isaac)
You shoot him?

ISAAC
Nope.

FRANK
(to Ellen)
You shoot him?

ELLEN
Why'd I do that? He'd the makings of a drover!

FRANK
(to John)
You shoot him?

JOHN
I was in bed.

FRANK
Anyone else? Elmer?

ELLEN
He's deaf.

FRANK
Well, there was a gun went off
in the night.
(he scans them all again)
You'd best lay him out and get a
box.

He and Isaac stand up.

FRANK
All right, we've labour to commence.

*Ellen and Elmira clear away dishes.
Michael and John haul Matthew
onto the table and lay him out, fold
his hands. Ellen puts a piece of candle in his hands.*

A BACK PASTURE —
OPEN FIELDS. EVENING.

The railway line, distant.
A herd of cows, Elmira
milking. The sky and
land colourless, the horizon vast, the pasture
stony and eaten down.
Latimer approaches in
work clothes — dirty
with chaff and dust. He
carries a scythe.

ELMIRA
You staying?

Latimer rests the scythe, examines his blistered hands.

LATIMER
Can I just ask you about this brother of yours — that, ah, deceased at the table ...

ELMIRA
Listen, you stayin or not?

LATIMER
Look, there's no question your family are fine people. Quite honestly I like them. You know, they're —

She gets up with the milk bucket.

ELMIRA
You're the first person ever said that.

LATIMER
Well, I mean they're all right.

Latimer takes the bucket from her.

ELMIRA
They're awful and you know it. Now I want to show you something.

THE RAILWAY TRACKS. EVENING.

Elmira, Latimer carrying the scythe and milk bucket. They walk the ties. The crickets loud and heavy.

ELMIRA
This railroad through here was the biggest windfall Granpa ever had. He took the company for a right fortune, rooked the contractor into building on this here wet land so's he could sell the whole right of way to him ... Only trouble is, every now'n agin you get the tracks sinkin down in the mire and it causes wrecks.
(pause)
We even had a few hired men tried to leave on this train ... But it was goin too fast.

REMOTE, LOWER COUNTRY. DAY.

Latimer and Elmira following a ruined fence line.

LATIMER
You know, there are buildings over five stories high down there, you can have a bath, you can go to the store. It's quite incredible.

ELMIRA
Remember, if anyone asks, I been milkin.

LATIMER
I mean, we could just leave on the six o'clock —

ELMIRA
I been tryin to leave this place myself for eighteen years now.

LATIMER
Odd, you don't look a day over twenty-six.

ELMIRA
I'm eighteen.

She looks around, then lowers her voice.

ELMIRA
Now listen good. They found that railroad money where Granpa told them, they think someone's shifted it and they are fit to kill.

DOWN BY THE DEAD ELMS. DAY.

Stark, towering dead elms in forlorn pasture. Latimer and Elmira sit down on a bank, resting the scythe and bucket. Elmira heaves her dress up over her thigh.

LATIMER
Don't you think the ground's a little rough here? Maybe we can —

ELMIRA
Here.

From the top of her stocking she pulls out a folded document which she opens.

ELMIRA
(reads)
My dearest Elmira, my estate, acquired from the railway, and the title deed to the property and all my possessions —

LATIMER
Oh good. It's in writing.

ELMIRA
(reading)
— are buried on this land at the farthest extent of the shadow cast by the second dead elm west from the creek on November 16th at 9:28 in the morning.

Latimer indicates a spot in the mid-distance.

LATIMER
That should fall ... about ... there, by that stone.

ELMIRA
They all think somebody's shifted it and they'll be watching each other and us til they go blind.

LATIMER
Get shovels down here tonight and we can —

ELMIRA
There won't be no time for guessing and digging around. We got to wait til November, get it on the fall of that shadow and get out while the getting's good. They'll kill to get their hands on it. I'm bein honest with you.

LATIMER
Or ... we could just go down to the city and come back.

ELMIRA
No.

She looks into his eyes.

ELMIRA

We'll both be watched because of last night.

(pause)

I don't want to stay here alone ...

Elmira leans against him, takes his arm. He fumbles toward her; his hand finds the hem of her dress, begins to move up her leg. She laughs, then catches his wrist, sits up.

ELMIRA

Shshshsh! ... There's someone down here, I swear!

They look around. The drowned elms, the low pasture, the rising bald land, the blasted fields, the fences. Stillness. Crickets chanting. She pulls his hand away and holds it.

ELMIRA

And we got to watch them too.

She moves her face close to his, looks into his eyes.

ELMIRA

You staying?

A HARROWED FIELD. DUSK.

A wind blows the last leaves from a stunted tree. A harrowed field blowing with dust, littered with ploughed-up stones. Latimer, white as a ghost with dust, staggers, nearly dropping a boulder as he tumbles it onto the flatbed of a horse-drawn stone-boat driven by Isaac. Elmer tosses a boulder twice its size. Michael throws a heavy stone to John who heaves it on. Latimer reels with fatigue.

THE RAWLINSON HOUSE. EVENING. FALL.

The house against an ash-grey dusk. Wild wind blowing. One light burning in the kitchen window.

THE RAWLINSON HOUSE. THE KITCHEN. NIGHT.

Frank at the table, very drunk, with an empty glass and half-empty bottle. A single kerosene lamp gutters.

FRANK
You black-guard ... I should just have done away with you when I had the chance, made a clean job of it.

We see that he is addressing no one.

FRANK
In fact you owe to me I didn't kill you, you parasitical sonofabitch ...

The outside door opens, behind him. He leaps up, almost jumping out of his skin, whirls around only to find his eldest son, Isaac, who has just come in.

ISAAC
You should be in bed.

FRANK
(pause)
I been wantin to talk to you ...

ISAAC
Yeah, well I've been ...

FRANK
This hired man come up here ... I don't like the look of him.

ISAAC
You hired him ...

FRANK
Since the day he come, there's been
trouble.

ISAAC
You knew what you were doin when
you hired him.

FRANK
Listen boy, you're my eldest ... You're
in line. You watch him.

ISAAC
Why don't you just go off and spend it all on cat-houses and liquor.

A train whistle blasts twice in the distance.

FRANK
Listen to me, boy, don't you —

*He stops, cut short by the whistle. There follows a silence, as if the sound had
evoked a common memory. Isaac stares at him steadily. The wind thunders around
the house.*

ISAAC
All them dreams he'd end by hangin.
(pause)
For fear is dealins with the railroad come to light.

*Frank seethes with loathing, suddenly explodes forward, pitching his drink in Isaac's
face. But Isaac has already seized a chair and all in one motion wings it over his head*

as Frank's hand plunges forward with an open jack-knife. The chair crashes down on Frank's head. All of this happens in under four seconds; we know it has happened before.

Just as suddenly, Frank and Isaac stand stalk still, at bay, Isaac calm, impassive, the jack-knife embedded in his shoulder, his jacket slowly soaking blood. He looks down at it.

ISAAC
(pause)
This is my only jacket.

He pulls the knife out, without flinching.

Frank looks at Isaac steadily, blood streaming down his face. Isaac slowly folds the jack-knife, hands it back to Frank.

FRANK
Son?

Isaac looks him in the eye.

FRANK
I'm glad we had this talk.

Isaac turns and slowly goes upstairs.

THE RAWLINSON HOUSE. THE BACK VERANDA. NIGHT.

Latimer opens the kitchen door quietly and goes in.

THE RAWLINSON HOUSE.
THE KITCHEN.

It is almost pitch dark. Latimer, covered with dust, crosses quietly to the stairs. Suddenly we hear a cough out of the darkness.

Latimer freezes, and slowly turns. A match is struck and flares, illuminating Frank's bloody face and the overturned chair as he lights a candle. Latimer starts, terrified as does Frank when he sees the dusty ghost-white apparition that is Latimer in the same illumination. They are both hollering.

FRANK
Arrrrrghgh!! It wasn't my fault! It wasn't my fault! I swear to God! Please!

LATIMER
I'm sorry! I'm sorry! I'm sorry!

FRANK
(pause, realising)
Oh it's you.

LATIMER
... Sorry, I ah, I just —

FRANK
Boy.
(pause)
I know what you're doing.
(pause)
Don't go thinking we're blind here.

Latimer surveys the chaos around the table. Frank looks around a little awkwardly, gestures vaguely.

FRANK
Sometimes I ah ... I like to sit up late ... mull things over ... But you mind no business but your own, here, boy, you understand ... ? Don't underestimate me ...

LATIMER
No ... On the contrary, sir, I —

FRANK
No, no, shut up. *(Frank slowly stands up.)* I know the world from A to Z. I been as far north as Magog and south all the way past Canaan. I been in terrible altercations in Scragtown and Armageddon. I've drank in Molesworth, I stabbed two men in Bayfield, so I've lived their culture there, and I can dock sheep, poll cattle, narble harness, treble pluck spring fowl for autumn dowsing and sickle the hames of tumbrils for picket-pulling, so there's not much escapes my notice. So boy, you better watch how you walk.

He picks up a bottle.

FRANK
There's a certain issue in regard of my late father and you're not to concern yourself with it.

He pours himself a drink.

FRANK
But if you know of anything that might be considered useful in regard to this encumbrance ...

He pours himself a second glass, picks up both drinks and approaches Latimer.

FRANK
... you come to me first, boy, and don't take no notice of the others. And then ... and only then ...

He downs his own drink.

FRANK
... we could perhaps come to some mutually profitable agreement ...

He is about to hand the other drink to Latimer, but downs that one as well.

FRANK
But you take advantage of anything you might find on this place, them fields will be the last thing you ever see.

A HARVESTED FIELD STOOKED WITH SHEAVES.
AUTUMN. MORNING.

A wagon stooked high with sheaves of grain driven through brown stubble by Elmer. John heaves up the sheaves with a fork, murmuring to no one in particular.

JOHN
Yeah ... When we ain't sleepin we're workin. We like to work ... Winter-time we set. Fridays we like to fight ...

Latimer with a fork pitching alongside him. Michael receiving and piling the sheaves on top. Ellen binds sheaves in the mid-distance. Latimer glances at John in irritation.

JOHN
If we ain't settin, sleepin or fightin, then we're workin again. Spring afore plantin, too warm to set, too cool to plant, we get to drankin, tear up the country, vandalise the hotels.

The wagon moves forward. Latimer crosses to the other side where he sees Elmira stooking sheaves. As Elmira moves on to build the next stook, Latimer finds himself walking parallel between her and the wagon, concealing them both. Elmira joins him but they keep moving.

LATIMER
You hear people up around the house last night?

Elmira
They don't sleep good.

Latimer
Well sometimes I think I'm having their dreams.

Elmira
If that was true, you wouldn't even blink for fear you'd fall asleep.

Elmira lags back and glances out behind the wagon.

Elmira
Get back working.

The wagon moves forward to reveal Isaac arriving at the reins of a team drawing an empty wagon.

LATIMER
When can I see you?

ELMIRA
Meet me at the dance on the 15th. The day after's the day we dig. Now get away. Remember, you're a hired hand.

LATIMER
What do you mean, 'hired hand?'

She moves on.

THE DEAD ELMS.

The dead elm, stark in dead pasture. Clouds are torn across the sky.
The shadow of the tree appears and dissipates.

THE BACK VERANDA OF THE RAWLINSON HOUSE.

A constable in a shabby old suit steps up to the kitchen door. In one hand he holds a sheaf of blue papers, with the other he draws a heavy revolver, cocks it, conceals it in his jacket again.

THE RAWLINSON KITCHEN.

Latimer and all the Rawlinsons save Elmer and Isaac eating breakfast. Elmira pours tea. Under the table, she slides her foot up Latimer's leg almost to his crotch. Latimer pauses, manages to maintain his composure. There is a knock at the door. Ellen crosses and opens it disclosing the constable.

CONSTABLE
Morning Ma'am, I've a warrant for the arrest of Elmer Rawlinson.

ELLEN
You're out of luck, he's shaving.

CONSTABLE
Could you please ask him to —

ELLEN
I told you, he's shaving.

CONSTABLE
(*shouts inside*)
I've also got seventy-six charges against the rest of you!

FRANK
(*shouts; his mouth full*)
We're harvesting!

CONSTABLE
We'll have to ask you to come quietly.

FRANK
I still got oats to take off, God damnit, are you mad? I'm not goin anywhere.

CONSTABLE
Well neither am I.

ELLEN
Then come in, have some porridge while you're here.

She turns away from the door. The constable comes in haltingly, slowly draws the revolver.

CONSTABLE
It'll be easier for everyone if you all come quietly.

Ellen moves to the stove, gets the porridge. John, Frank and Michael look up with contemptuous indifference. The constable waves the revolver back and forth uncertainly. This will probably be too much for him. Ellen puts his porridge on the table.

ELLEN
(shouts)
Sit down, Lord love a duck, I gone to the trouble!

Warily, the constable puts the revolver back in his jacket and sits down. Isaac comes in from the veranda.

ISAAC
Morning, constable.

CONSTABLE
(raising a spoonful of porridge)
You're under arrest.

ISAAC
How's the wife?

CONSTABLE
She had a hysterical pregnancy. You're charged with assault and arson.

ELLEN
(yells)
You going to eat your porridge or not?

The constable tastes it, can barely keep it down. Elmer comes down the stairs.

CONSTABLE
Long time to be shaving.

ELLEN
They start from above the ears.

CONSTABLE
(to Elmer)
You're under arrest.

Elmer crosses and holds his hand out to the constable.

ELMER
How do you do?

The constable shakes Elmer's hand haltingly.

CONSTABLE
Insulting and abusive language and shooting with intent.

ISAAC
That wasn't him, it was me. He done the vandalism behind Maley's barber shop and the arson on the town hall.

CONSTABLE
Lord love a duck, everyone said it was Mick Sweeney.

ISAAC
No wonder there ain't law and order around here with likes of you.

The constable looks at his watch and stands up.

CONSTABLE
Look, are you comin or not?

The Rawlinsons go on eating.

THE VERANDA.

The constable comes out, steps down. About twenty farmers gathered in the lane with pitchforks, a shotgun, a couple of rifles.

CONSTABLE
They won't come.

The farmers murmur among themselves, slowly turn and shuffle off.

THE RAWLINSON HOUSE. THE KITCHEN. NIGHT.

Elmira, in a dim pool of light ascends the staircase with a kerosene lamp. She stops and listens to the low thunder of the Rawlinsons snoring.

She passes down the upstairs corridors, doors ajar to a low, muffled murmuring.

A BEDROOM. NIGHT.

Michael and John in their beds in odd postures — Michael, his leg crossed up in the air, John rocking back and forth violently.

MICHAEL
(in his sleep)
... Get in the ground or bury mother afore the thresher ...
(louder)
What you say?

JOHN
(in his sleep)
I said Hiram found his way to the basin on top of the month.

THE CORRIDOR. NIGHT.

Elmira opens her door.

ELMIRA'S ROOM. NIGHT.

She turns, closing the door as she sets down the lamp. Out of the darkness the voice of her old brother:

ISAAC
Good-day.

She starts and turns, the lamp throw-ing light on Isaac sitting on a chair drunk, in disarray, with a loosened tie, a bowler hat perched on the back of his head and a bouquet of wilted flowers.

ELMIRA
Oh Jesus, you scared me.

ISAAC
You talkin to that hired man?

ELMIRA
(patronizing)
Look at you. Now stop that fool-ishness and go to bed.

ISAAC
I got these flowers.

He tosses them onto a table.

ISAAC
You going to the dance?

ELMIRA
I doubt it, now get on to bed.

ISAAC
Is he going?
(pause)
I know where to get that money. It ain't where you think.

ELMIRA
(smiles)
And where do I think it is?

Isaac gets up, comes close to her, lowers his voice.

ISAAC
I can get that money, get you off of this place, so's you never get to look at it again. And the old man can go hang.

ELMIRA
Can you now?

Clumsily but softly he touches her arm. She edges back.

THE WEST BEDROOM. NIGHT.

Latimer, in long johns, with one ear to the wall. He can hear their voices murmuring. It is followed by laughter and some sort of fumbling, a chair falling over; more laughter. Latimer straightens uneasily. There is a short silence followed by footsteps and the door closing.

A GRIST MILL DAY.

The loading dock. Wagons drawn up, piled high with sacks of grain. Mill workers move about, hauling and moving sacks. Isaac and Latimer unloading sacks from the Rawlinson Wagon.

LATIMER
Isn't there some dance in Canaan, tonight?

Isaac doesn't answer.

LATIMER
Just wondering if you were
going.

ISAAC
I'm workin.

LATIMER
Does anyone go to the
dances?

ISAAC
You ever touch a woman?

LATIMER
Did I ever what?

The dock. The mill owner appears, looks at them and shouts:

MILL OWNER
I told you, you can't use this mill!

Isaac looks at him briefly, continues working. The owner comes over quickly.

MILL OWNER
Go on, get out. You're not grindin here.

Latimer looks up, stands back.

ISAAC
Keep working.

Isaac suddenly shoulders into the mill owner.

ISAAC
What's that you say, Jack?

MILL OWNER
You want to use this mill, damn well pay your bills.

Out in the road about thirty passers-by have gathered. They know what's afoot.

ISAAC
Then go over to Harrison's grist mill, tell them to take our grain.

MILL OWNER
Harrison's burned down.

The crowd watches in dead silence.

ISAAC
Now I just wonder why on earth that would be.

He glares at the mill owner. The mill owner steps back. Isaac shoulders a bag of oats. Latimer follows suit.

INSIDE THE GRIST MILL. DAY.

The hopper. The belts, chutes, wheels thundering. Isaac and Latimer hauling grain sacks to the hopper. Isaac slits them with a jack-knife. Latimer dumps them.

ISAAC
I asked you, you ever touch a woman?

LATIMER
How do you mean, "touch"?

The floor is cramped and dim, dust hanging in the air, poorly lit by windows fogged with cobwebs. They have to shout over the din.

ISAAC
I touched one Tuesday when I went up to slaughter hogs in Armageddon.

LATIMER
You what?

ISAAC
Nobody never tell you bout "touching". Where children come from and all?

LATIMER
What are you talking about?

ISAAC
Come over here, boy.

Isaac crosses the mill floor still holding the open jack-knife and stops in a corner foggily lit by a window, Latimer follows.

ISAAC
It's called fornication.

LATIMER
You mean —

ISAAC
How old are you?

LATIMER
Thirty-one, why?

ISAAC
You don't know bout that? I'll be damned.

LATIMER
What are you — ?

ISAAC
First the man and woman get dressed. The man puts on a Sunday suit, gets a bunch of flowers, and the woman puts on a dress and they go out in a buggy. That's the fore-play. Then they go to some bushes. The man pulls down his suspenders and then —

LATIMER
I know that. I know. What are you — ?

ISAAC
And then he gets all hard, and the woman pulls up her dress and she's all ready to get on with him, right? That's the second part.

A SIDEROAD. MASKINONGE.

Isaac at the reins driving the empty wagon. Latimer beside him.

ISAAC
And they're still at it. And they're just ruttin' and ruttin' and a-heavin' away.

65

LATIMER
Look, I don't really need to hear all this —

Isaac turns the team into a wagon track through pasture. They approach a farmstead from the rear.

ISAAC
And they're down there in all the dirt and the chaff and the whole thing's just right filthy and he's inside her and he's just a-pumpin away like a steam thresher and she's a-squealin like a hog.

THE FARMSTEAD. BARN AND BUILDINGS.

Latimer and Isaac approaching the barn, the wagon parked behind them. Isaac is carrying a large can.

ISAAC
Now they're gettin to the evil part, the original sin, the actual fornication.

The barn door is ajar. Isaac carries the can through, Latimer follows.

THE BARN. THE HAY LOFT. DAY.

Farm wealth: sheaves, hay, straw, implements. Isaac splashes kerosene from the can all over the straw on the floor.

LATIMER
What are you doing?

Isaac lights a match and tosses it, igniting the barn floor.

ISAAC
Boundary dispute.

(he turns to Latimer)

So then the man lets go of his seed inside the woman. And that's what does it, that's the filth that begets humanity and the woman gets all big and they drop it off at some church somewhere and it just adds to the world's suffering and the endless round of iniquity. But the thing is, everybody keeps doin it, what you make of that, eh? And I'm the worst, I can't stop doin it myself and I done dropped children in Magog and Gehenna. So I'm beginnin to reckon even *you*, even you maybe done it too.

Latimer backs away from the flames.

LATIMER
I don't know what this is about.

ISAAC
It's about my sister. You got a yen for her, I can tell.

THE SIDEROAD.

Isaac driving the wagon, Latimer beside him. Behind them, in the receding distance, the barn going up in an inferno, the column of smoke into the sky.

ISAAC
(after a silence)
You so much as touch her, you'll never know what hit you.

LATIMER
There seems to be some confusion here.

ISAAC
Not about my brother Matthew.

LATIMER
That died? I was upstairs that night, I —

Isaac stops the wagon, seizes him by the collar.

ISAAC
I got brothers who'll testify unless I get that railroad money.

With his other hand, Isaac shoves a knife to Latimer's throat. It draws a trickle of blood.

LATIMER
You're getting blood on my shirt.

ISAAC
And until then you ain't gettin off the property in one piece. And if you so much as try, I can get Elmira just as easy.

THE BACK PASTURE.

The dead elm against the western sky.

A TAVERN IN CANAAN.

An ornate bar, mirror, battered tables and chairs, spit-stained floors, game heads on the walls. Five or six men, ageless, dim and dangerous in dark suits seated in a row against the wall. Against the opposite wall, a row of women, grim opposite numbers to the men. For the moment we might think it was a funeral reception. But suddenly rough and itinerant hobo musicians on mandolin, banjo, guitar and fiddle strike up the lame and creaking sounds of the *Crowley Waltz*. Couples lurch and stagger into the floor.

THE MAIN STREET OF CANAAN.

A short wide thoroughfare. Stark ramshackle shops. The high, monolithic brick front of the hotel and tavern whence the archaic squeal of the *Crowley Waltz*, shouting, breaking glass. A tangle of horses and buggies parked. Latimer in a dark suit, no tie, stops outside, looks around uneasily.

THE ROAD INTO CANAAN.

Elmira drives a buggy, Ellen beside her. They are dressed in mourning — the clothes they use to go to the dance.

ELLEN
The Crandall brothers'll be at the dance. I heard they got eyes for you.

Elmira dreads this recurring discussion.

ELLEN
Just wondered if you met anyone you'd set your cap for.

ELMIRA
What, in Maskinonge?

ELLEN
Ain't nowhere else.

ELMIRA
No one.

ELLEN
Ain't nothin you'd call a man nowhere else. I should know, I been up as far as Ingersoll, there's nothing up there.
(pause)
A woman wants a man can look after himself, a man what's sober, industrious and self-sufficient unto himself.

ELMIRA
Is that what you got?

ELLEN
Just don't be leadin all manner of people on.

ELMIRA
And what, pray tell, is all manner of people?

ELLEN
All manner of insubstantial people from outside the township.

ELMIRA
Like what?

ELLEN
You know like what. I seen you talking to him.

ELMIRA
What are you on about?

ELLEN
The hired man, who else?

THE TAVERN. THE BAR-ROOM. NIGHT.

Murky, infernal in kerosene light. Wild, bawdy laughter, loud talk
as the music cranks on, the floor soaked with beer and broken glass.
Dancing couples jostling. Men are packed along the bar. Half a
dozen side-road ruffians waiting to start something. Latimer makes
his way through the crowd. He passes two men assisting a third, his
face streaming blood.

THE MAIN STREET OF CANAAN.

Ellen and Elmira driving in, in the buggy.

ELLEN
Where else are you going to meet people?

ELMIRA
(pause)
I seen you talkin to the hired man yourself.

ELLEN
Not me. But between you and him there's no loss of words.

ELMIRA
If he asks, I show him where things are.

ELLEN
I'll bet you show him where things are.

Elmira pulls the buggy to a sudden halt. They are within earshot of the cacophony at the dance.

ELMIRA
What do you think you're implyin? Eh? What?

ELLEN
Our farm is not a brothel.

THE TAVERN.

The atmosphere is now entirely charged with alcohol. Couples dancing and men fighting intermixed; patches of floor slippery with blood. Brawlers pulled apart by the crowd, everyone heaving until they crash into the bar. The music grinding on. Latimer sqeezed in at the bar with a drink. He surveys the crowd, strains to see the door.

A BACK STREET. EVENING.

The noise of the dance muted, beyond. In the darkness, Isaac, John, Michael and Elmer stagger along drunk, laughing, two of them carrying bottles. A bottle thrown and smashed.

THE TAVERN.

Ellen and Elmira pull into the tangle of parked buggies. They approach the steps and gallery, passing through drunken, loitering men.

ELLEN
There's John Sutherland. I've heard tell he has eyes for you. Now that's a fine figure of a man.

John Sutherland stands apart, thin, shabby and cold sober, counting out change in the palm of his hand.

ELLEN
He's a good Presbyterian pig butcher, he scrapes cow hides for extra cash and he don't drink, he's as dry as a whistle.

ELMIRA
I think the competition'd be too great.

THE TAVERN.

Arguing, fighting, yelling — the dance continues, the music grinding on. Latimer searching the crowd. He glimpses Ellen and Elmira. The two women push through. They are jostled. Elmira uses the opportunity to slip away from Ellen. Elmira edges through the crowd, moves closer to the dance floor. Someone takes her arm from behind. She whirls, about to strike, finds herself facing Latimer. He is drunk.

LATIMER
Dance?

She bursts out laughing.

ELMIRA
You're drunk!

She cannot disguise her delight. They move into a clumsy waltz. Elmira involuntarily caresses his back. He nuzzles her ear. She laughs. This, ironically, is their moment alone.

ELMIRA
You can't stay long. My mother's here.

Ellen and a few big, dangerous old women surveying the crowd grimly.

Latimer and Elmira turn on the dance floor, very close.

ELMIRA
Tomorrow's the sixteenth. The day the shadow falls. You watch me in the morning for a sign.

They are jostled, the dancers partially cleared as two bloody men roll onto the floor.

LATIMER
What's the trouble here anyway?

ELMIRA
It's just a dance. Why?

It finally dissolves into a full-scale brawl. A knife is drawn. Five men engaged in pummelling, kicking, eye-gouging, hair-pulling, biting, vicious and homicidal. Until one of the fighters rears up holding a knife and a table leg, staring toward the door in horror. His opponent, following his gaze scrambles backward. The music stops. The others, look up, all of them backing away as the crowd withdraws as well. Silence. The whole tavern staring toward the door.

There stand Elmer, Isaac, John and Michael surveying the scene. In the crowd, Elmira yanks Latimer by the arm, whispers:

ELMIRA
Get home, you'll have to walk, I'm sorry. Go out by the back. Quick.

Latimer sidles out toward the back.

MICHAEL
Why's it so quiet?

ELMER
Anybody seen a city boy here?

The Rawlinson brothers suddenly erupt in mocking laughter.

CUSTOMER
He just left.

ISAAC
The hell he did.

CANAAN. A BACK STREET.

Latimer moving along quickly on foot to the sound of the tavern erupting in a riot behind him.

THE RAWLINSON HOUSE. KITCHEN.

Frank half dressed, lit by a candle in his hand.

FRANK
Who's that?

Nothing before him but deep shadows. He moves to the corridor.

FRANK
Come back here!

He rushes the darkness, sees something disappear, subliminally. The sound of a door slamming.

A SIDE ROAD. MASKINONGE.

Latimer walking quickly in moonlight. He glances behind him. The moon above silver and full.

THE RAWLINSON HOUSE.
THE KITCHEN.

The corridor. Frank emerges, hollers:

FRANK
You sonofabitch!

A bedroom door flies open disclosing Ellen.

ELLEN
We come in late, I'm tryin to sleep. Who you talking to?

FRANK
Someone was in the house!

ELLEN
You're mad. You got a bottle in here?

Frank turns on her, brays with laughter.

FRANK
Bah! There hasn't been a bottle in this house in fifteen years!

She comes up to him face to face.

ELLEN
I can smell it.

FRANK
You've had too much Bible, that's what you've had.

ELLEN
Who you talkin to in here?

FRANK
Get to bed. Leave me alone.

ELLEN
(pause)
Well, he's dead anyway.

FRANK
Who's dead?

ELLEN
Your father.

They stare at each other through twenty years' hatred.

ELLEN
I'd have a half a dollar for a pair of shoes if you was half the man your dad was.

With a lightning reflex he kicks her hard in the shin with a loud, vicious crack. She stares at him steadily without flinching, smiles.

FRANK
You ought to *have* a half a dollar the way you conspired with him.

Ellen gives out a laugh and turns away.

THE RAWLINSON PROPERTY. THE LANE.

Latimer arrives to find the house dark, silent, asleep. He looks up and sees the moon just as it recedes behind dark cloud — casting the house into the thickest obscurity.

THE RAWLINSON HOUSE. THE KITCHEN.

The veranda door; the room in darkness. Latimer comes in. He makes his way toward the staircase. There is a slight knock. He stops, listens, moves again. And again there is a sound. He looks around at the corridor, the staircase, the kitchen — all in darkness. He takes another footstep — and there seems to be another footfall almost on top of his own.

In a threshold a boot falls. Latimer moves to the hallway, passes the threshold, an axe flies down in an arc into the doorjamb right in front of his face. He leaps backward. A figure lunges at him through the doorway. Latimer stumbles backward though the kitchen chairs into the table. The shadow rushes him wielding the axe; he leaps, stumbles into the downstairs bedroom corridor, turns. He tears into the corridor catching the figure in vague silhouette. He catches a doorknob, thrusts it open.

AN EMPTY ROOM.

He leaps in, slamming the door, turning only to see a door in the opposite corner burst open with another form lunging after him, perhaps the same one. He tears back out.

THE KITCHEN.

He finds the corridor clear, heads for the kitchen when he's suddenly blocked by the same or another shadow with an axe. They collide, piling into the kitchen. Indecipherable chaos. A wild struggle, the axe, perhaps two axes, rising and falling, splintering into furniture. Heaving bodies, two, perhaps four. Axes, bodies, feet, arms, sundering furniture. A gun blast and lick of flame explodes in the darkness. Latimer lunges for the stairs, scrambles up.

THE UPSTAIRS CORRIDOR.

Pitch black. He feels his way, turns a corner, stops breathless and listens. He can hear the crashing unabated, below. He lets himself into his room, slams the bolt.

THE RAWLINSON PROPERTY.

House and out-buildings. Utter bleakness, a stormy and lurid sunrise. The baleful cock-crow warns of another day.

THE RAWLINSON HOUSE. THE KITCHEN.

Everyone is seated in their usual places for breakfast. The room is a shambles; splintered wood, broken chairs moved aside, broken crockery. All the Rawlinsons, save for Elmira, are battered — abrasions, cuts, swelling, dried blood. They eat in ruminative silence. The light is preternatural, reddish — a sunset at sunrise, as if time were running backward. Latimer looks up at the wall calendar; the day is the 16th, the day when the shadow must fall.

In the distance, the train whistle hoots twice followed by the distant roar of the Maskinonge Central; and then, quite suddenly a terrible screaming of iron against iron and a tremendous, extended crashing of passenger and freight cars, an explosion and gushing of steam, followed by hissing. All the Rawlinsons get briskly to their feet.

FRANK
Maskinonge Central.

They all put on their coats.

ELLEN
It's late today.

ISAAC
(to John)
Go get the wrecking bar and all the sacks.

They all go out. Latimer is uncertain; he looks to Elmira who is putting on her coat. Elmira nods to him to follow.

A FIELD.

Latimer and Elmira move quickly with shovels.

ELMIRA
With luck they'll be out at the wreck all morning.

LATIMER
Someone tried to kill me with an axe last night.

ELMIRA
It's cause you came in late.

THE RAILWAY TRACKS.

The wreck; the toppled locomotive, the long furrow of churned-up turf, twisted rails, splintered ties; passenger cars jack-knifed, steaming and smoking. Passengers scattered, staggering, moaning. Elmer and Michael sifting through scattered luggage and debris. Elmer picks a pocket watch off a man lying prostrate against broken siding. Thunder rumbles.

THE DEAD ELMS. A RIVER BANK.

Half sun; thunderheads rolling in. Latimer and Elmira crouch with shovels under a river bank. The dead elm stands forlornly. Latimer pulls out his pocket watch. It reads 9:15.

ELMIRA
I know it's down here. It's in Granpa's old packing case. I swear it is.

Latimer scans the sky, inky with darkness and thunder.

LATIMER
All we got to have is bright sun in five minutes.

Thunder crashes, lightning strikes.

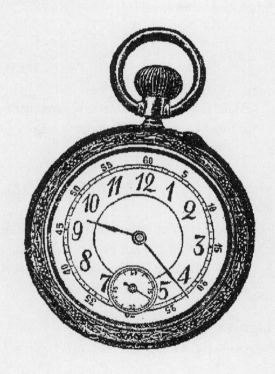

LATIMER
So if the clouds suddenly evaporate and no one moves the money and we get off here without being killed, we're scot free.

Elmira pulls him close.

ELMIRA
Look, it's enough that you stayed.

Just as she hugs him, light washes over them. Latimer looks at his watch: it reads 9:28. He looks up to see a fracture in the cloud cover, light breaking. A shaft of platinum cuts across the land, throwing the shadow of the elm. Latimer hurls himself forward, sprints to the end of the elm's shadow, spears his shovel down at the farthest point at the very moment the shadow fades and the land darkens again.

The elm looms against the brooding sky. In the pasture, Latimer and Elmira dig furiously in pouring rain.

THE TRAIN WRECK.

Frank and Ellen working with a crowbar and axe to dislodge a piece of freight car siding. Thunder crashes, rain pours down.

THE DEAD ELMS.

Pouring rain. Latimer and Elmira knee-deep in the hole they've dug, now scraping at a surface with their shovels. Struggling, they dislodge something, and haul out a beaten, dirty steamer trunk. Latimer looks at her. He is beside himself.

LATIMER
I guess I've got to apologize. I can't believe it.

They kiss in the downpour.

ELMIRA
I told you, didn't I?

LATIMER
But didn't I believe you?

ELMIRA
I don't know if you did or not.

LATIMER
I had to.

She pulls his hand to her breast, then stops him.

ELMIRA
Wait.

LATIMER
For what?

ELMIRA
Til we open it. Then we can celebrate.

LATIMER
There isn't time. They're going to wonder.

ELMIRA
The wreck'll keep them.

They look at the case which seems luminous. Slowly, Latimer gets to his knees, swings the shovel, breaking an old rusty padlock.

They look inside. For a long time their faces do not change. In the trunk are human remains — a corpse dressed much as Latimer was upon his arrival.

ELMIRA
That's Hiram Bradley.

LATIMER
The sewing machine salesman ...

ELMIRA
Oh my God ...

LATIMER
I am not jealous.

ELMIRA
My Granpa didn't kill him ... someone
else did.

Latimer turns to her.

LATIMER
Look —

*She is staring at the corpse. She reaches down. A dog-eared Bible sits in the crook
of its arm.*

LATIMER
Don't touch it.

ELMIRA
That's the Bible that Hiram took, the one Granpa give me.

She picks it up.

LATIMER
Leave it.

ELMIRA
Wait. There's a ribbon-marker.

LATIMER
Let's just get that back in the ground and get to hell off here before anyone
sees it.

She opens it.

ELMIRA
There's a passage marked: Genesis 19, verse 26. "But Lot's wife looked back from behind him, and she became a pillar of salt. And Abraham got up early in the morning to the place ... " — and then someone's written in with pencil — "the place that was 17 feet due west of the 77th railroad tie from the south boundary going to Gomorrah Station."

LATIMER
How witty.

ELMIRA
(points)
Gomorrah station's up that way. That'd be in the south-east field.

LATIMER
No! There's frost in the ground now, John's ploughing in that field and by the time he's done it'll be frozen solid til April. There isn't the time.

ELMIRA
Sure we have the time.

LATIMER
What time? Til we get killed?

ELMIRA
Til April.

Latimer looks at Elmira, speechless.

LATIMER
Are you mad? That's the whole winter!

ELMIRA
What's one winter? I been here eighteen years.

Latimer quickly begins shovelling the earth back into the hole.

LATIMER
You can stay with my family in the city.

ELMIRA
I'm not bein somebody's servin girl.

LATIMER
Well that's what I've been doing here.

Elmira is not listening, she is thinking.

ELMIRA
Look, we know where Hiram's body is and if someone else here has gone hid that money, we just might get it out of them by threatening to go to the law.

LATIMER
That's blackmail.

ELMIRA
You're right. It's too dangerous.

LATIMER
Look, you coming with me or not?

Elmira turns and looks at him.

ELMIRA
You remember saying you loved me?

LATIMER
That I what?

ELMIRA
That you loved —

LATIMER
That's not the point!

ELMIRA
Or you just come here gold-digging like them others?

LATIMER
Yes — ! I mean no! I asked you to come back *with* me, didn't I?

ELMIRA
You saying there's a limit? I'm only worth it this far?

LATIMER
Look, I love you. But I really, really hate your family.

ELMIRA
And you're right. And they'll be fit to kill and they'll be watching each other and us til they go blind and it was them drove my Granpa to his death and that alone is enough reason to stay.
(she pulls him toward her)
You think about what we'll do the day we get off here.

LATIMER
You really take me for a fool, don't you?

THE RAWLINSON HOUSE. WINTER

The house and buildings in a howling blizzard.

THE RAWLINSON HOUSE. THE KITCHEN.

Latimer, in resignation, sitting idle with the Rawlinsons. Ellen in her rocking chair, almost comatose. Frank, Elmer, Isaac, Michael, John, Elmira seated round the stove all dressed in overlapping coats and scarves. Sporadic coughing, sniffling, sneezing. Noses drip. The wind thunders, shaking the windows.

Ellen opens an eye, looking sidelong at Frank who looks sidelong at Isaac who looks sidelong at Elmer who is asleep.

FRANK
What's the time?

ELLEN
Still a quarter past two.

MICHAEL
That's what it was in December.

Elmer stands up. Every one starts, suddenly watching him. He yawns, scratches himself.

ELLEN
Likely when the clock stopped.

He sits down and closes his eyes. They all fall back to dozing. Daylight fades to night.

THE RAWLINSON HOUSE. THE KITCHEN.

Daylight rises on the same scene: everyone sleeping. We hear the cock crow. The light increases.

Frank opens one eye, scans the room. John opens his eyes; finding himself watched by Ellen, he quickly feigns sleep. Slowly they all waken, coughing and sniffling. Ellen rises stiffly, coughing, and crosses to the stove and puts firewood in. Frank is now scanning a newspaper. Ellen crosses back to her chair.

ELLEN
(to Frank)
Who died?

FRANK
Read it yourself.

ELLEN
I can't read.
(pause)
Well?

FRANK
Neither can I ... Elmira, read the paper.

He tosses the paper across to Elmira. She picks it up, settles back and reads the front page.

FRANK
(hollers)
Aloud! Read it aloud!

ELMIRA
"A farmer hangs himself in his barn. An epidemic of insanity in Maryville. McPhail's barn is burned."

She glances at Latimer who gazes emptily.

FRANK
Whose arson was that? Was that ours?

MICHAEL
Yeah.

FRANK
Who did it?

MICHAEL
I did it.

Latimer stirs, glances over at Elmira. Elmira looks back to her paper but hitches her dress to show part of her stockinged leg and petticoat. Latimer is aroused. He closes his eyes.

ELMIRA
"Strychnine is the best way to deal with difficult mortgage payments and other bank debts."

FRANK
Read that one.

ELMIRA
That's all it says.

Latimer looks at Elmira, aroused. Ellen watches Elmira.

ELLEN
Foreign news.

ELMIRA
(pause)
"A man falls off a ladder in Kentucky. A woman has hysterics in New York. A farmer hangs himself in France."

FRANK
What was his name?

ELMIRA
(with difficulty)
Jean-Pierre Charpentier of Clermont Ferrand.

ELLEN
We don't know nobody in France.

Isaac is staring at Latimer. Latimer meets his gaze, looks away.

THE STABLE.

Latimer, heavily dressed, pitching manure. He hears something, stops, looks up. There is a swishing a rhythmic thumping on the loft floor above. He continues forking manure, looks up again, to see chaff falling down from the cracks between the floor-boards. He heads for the loft stairs, stops, listens again. But now there is only silence. He is about to go up when suddenly the loft door opens. Latimer darts back, concealing himself in a bull-pen as he watches Isaac come down, casually brushing chaff out of his hair as he passes. Latimer watches him pass out of view then climbs the stairs.

THE LOFT.

Latimer emerges from the top of the stairs and steps into the loft to the same swishing and thumping. It is Elmira clearing straw with a stable broom.

ELMIRA
What are you doing up here?

LATIMER
I was going to ask you the same question.

He goes up to her.

ELMIRA
Keep your voice down.

LATIMER
Wherever you are, he's nearby.

ELMIRA
I'm trying to find if he knows anything. Otherwise that Bible's all we got.

LATIMER
Can't he get himself a lady-friend in town?

ELMIRA
Once in a while, but they charge money. Give me a hand with this straw. This floor's rotten, it's got be repaired.

Latimer takes a fork and begins to clear the remaining area.

LATIMER
So what are you two doing all the time?

THE STABLE.

The ceiling is beginning to give way under their combined weight, unbeknownst to Isaac and Elmer as they feed the draft horses.

THE LOFT.

Latimer and Elmira clearing straw.

ELMIRA
He's just gotta be humoured, that's all.

LATIMER
Is *that* what they call it?

ELMIRA
You want to talk like that, you can just forget about the money and get out.

THE STABLE.

The loft floorboards begin to give way just as Isaac and Elmer go out, leaving the stable.

THE LOFT.

Latimer and Elmira pitching straw when there is a loud crack and the floor gives way beneath them.

THE STABLE.

The boards sunder and splinter as the two crash downward in a shower of straw and rotten wood and into a pen of uncleared manure — Latimer tumbling face-down on top of Elmira. They freeze. Latimer moves to get up, but Elmira seizes him, holds him.

ELMIRA
Shshshsh!

But the stable is empty. They lie still.

LATIMER
What I'm trying to say is, there's no money.

ELMIRA
Listen, my Granpa loved me. They can't get away with this.

LATIMER
And at the rate we're going, we're going to end up like them. Suspicious and murderous with our minds rotting. When we could just leave in the night.

He begins to get up. She stops him again.

ELMIRA
Shshsh! There's someone! Don't move!
(*silence*)
It was the wind.

He tries to get up again. She pulls him down.

ELMIRA
Don't move. Wait til we're sure.

She pulls him down and they kiss suddenly and heavily when suddenly there are remote voices and a door opening. She pushes him away.

ELMIRA
Go on, quick! Get out!

He insists a little, she pushes him. He gets to his feet.

THE RAWLINSON HOUSE. WINTER. DUSK.

The Rawlinsons, Elmira, Latimer once again gathered around the stove, semi-conscious. The light fades to twilight and there is a knock at the door. Everyone wakens with a fright, looking up. They are all afraid to open it. The knock comes again. They start again. Elmira gets up quickly, quietly lights a lamp.

Ellen rises silently, opens a drawer, pulls out a revolver. She goes and opens the door, she trains the revolver at an old tramp in a slouch-hat and overgrown beard coated with ice.

TRAMP
Paper, Ma'am?

She lowers the gun in her apron.

ELLEN
Free Press or the Advertiser?

The tramp puts his hand into a bag, pulls out a handful of scraps. Everyone stares from behind Ellen.

TRAMP
Scrap paper.

ELLEN
No thank you.

TRAMP
Bits of wire? Scraps of broken stove pipe? I got an end bracket broke off a window-blind, five cents. How bout cobwebs?

ELLEN
We got all that.

She begins to close the door.

TRAMP
Mildew? Foot and a half of wallpaper, slightly water-stained. Twelve cents.

ELLEN
I'll take it for seven.

TRAMP
You can have it for ten.

Ellen pulls a dime from her apron. The tramp hands over a torn end of wallpaper. She closes the door.

FRANK
Who was that bastard? What did he want? He was after something!

ELLEN
He was after nothin'! You're out of your mind!

THE RAWLINSON HOUSE.

Stark and gloomy. Snow drifted to the windows. A wind blowing. One light burns dimly in a downstairs window.

THE RAWLINSON HOUSE. THE UPSTAIRS CORRIDOR.

The top of the stairs. Latimer ascends, carrying a lamp. He moves down the corridor, pauses. Elmira's door is ajar and he can see her pulling off her bodice, naked from the waist up. She moves out of sight. He moves on to his room, almost driven mad.

THE RAWLINSON HOUSE. THE KITCHEN.

It is in almost complete darkness. The floorboards creak. A figure becomes discernible.

FRANK
All right, who are you?
(*it is Frank.*)
What do you want here?

He suddenly lurches, leaps across the room.

FRANK
Got you! I got you! Where are you?!

He rushes, tears round through the kitchen, the corridor, crashing past furniture, stumbling, scrambling as if he were losing something just beyond his grasp. His red-rimmed eyes dart, his face twitches, sweating. All we can hear is the thundering of the wind.

THE WEST BEDROOM.

Latimer in bed, reading by lamp-light. The wick gutters. He picks up the lamp. There is hardly any oil left. He tilts it, enlarging the flame.

THE KITCHEN. .

Absolute darkness. Frank is suddenly revealed in the glow of a lantern which he lights on the table. He is holding a crowbar. He crouches down, examines the floorboards. He works the crowbar very carefully in between a couple of planks. Quietly, painstakingly he raises one plank and then another, shifts them aside. He is almost afraid to go further. He looks around and with trembling hands reaches down between the planks. There, in the hiding space, is a bottle of liquor. He pulls it out, uncorks it and takes a long, gulping swallow, replaces the boards. He stands up holding the bottle; out of breath he hears a sound, jumps out of his skin, whirls and sees Isaac coming in from outside, closing the door. Isaac sees Frank gaunt, crazed, clutching the bottle.

FRANK
You could knock. You got no sense of decorum?

Isaac crosses to the stairs. Frank follows him, pulls him back.

FRANK
He's still here.

ISAAC
Who?

FRANK
The hired man.

ISAAC
So?

FRANK
Anyone in his right mind would have quit by now. Why's he still here?

ISAAC
Same reason everyone else is still here. What other reason is there?

FRANK
Eh?

ISAAC
The only reason you'd keep a shiftless bugger like that on this long is to have an outsider to lay the blame on.

THE WEST BEDROOM. NIGHT.

Latimer in bed. He has Bradley's Bible, and he's studying the passage from Genesis. The lamp-light guttering again. Wind kicks up, thunders outside; the window rattles. The draft blows out the lamp. Latimer gets out of bed, picks up the lamp.

THE KITCHEN.

Frank and Isaac stand face to face.

FRANK
Listen to me, boy. My father called me to his bedside.

ISAAC
Why, to take his bed pan?

FRANK
If you knew how much he loved me.

ISAAC
He'd sooner of given that money to the Pope. Why else would you go up to his room afore he died and threaten to tell the law about his dealings with the railroad if not to pry the sole right of inheritance out of him!

FRANK
(hisses)
Why ... you —

ISAAC
I'd hang myself too, rather than write you into my will.

FRANK
What!

ISAAC
Elmira found him with a rope round his neck.

Frank spits with sudden vehemence in Isaac's face.

FRANK
You liar!

Latimer begins to descend the stairs with the empty lamp when he hears the snarling and arguing. He steps back, flattens himself in the shadows and listens.

Frank and Isaac still glaring. Frank seizes Isaac by the jacket and shoves him against the wall.

FRANK
Let me tell you something, my lad. If and when that money comes to light, so help me God, you're not going to see a red cent of it in my life or after, because you want to know something?
(pause)
You're no kin to me nor nobody else here.
(pause)
You was dropped in a church and we picked you up and we took yous on as hired help.

Next to them is the stovepipe which bends and follows the ceiling before it disappears into the floor above.

ELMIRA'S ROOM.

Elmira in her night dress, leaning toward the stovepipe where it passes up through her floor and up the wall. She is listening as it carries the voices up from the kitchen.

THE KITCHEN.

Frank and Isaac staring at each other in silence.

FRANK
(at length)
You're just an employee and that's all you ever were.

He laughs. Isaac smiles.

FRANK
And the others, they all come from different litters too. But even they got more lineage than you.

At the top of the stairs, Latimer listens. He glances down the hall, now wondering about Elmira and Isaac.

THE RAWLINSON HOUSE.

The house is almost lost in a blizzard from hell.

THE RAWLINSON HOUSE. THE KITCHEN.

Latimer and the Rawlinsons are seated as before, gathered about the stove. But now their eyes are red-rimmed, faces worn and bloodless. Frank's eyes burning with insanity. Elmira picks up the Bible and glances at Latimer. Latimer looks away to see Isaac staring at him. Isaac looks at Elmira. Elmira avoids his glance, looks back to Latimer, to see Latimer staring at her. She picks up the newspaper with one hand and wedges the Bible in her skirts between her thighs with the other.

ELMIRA
We're in the papers again ... "The Rawlinsons, men of terrible aspect, are believed to stop at nothing to have satisfaction and revenge."

FRANK
That's not fair.

JOHN
We ain't done nothin since November.

FRANK
What's it say? "Men of terrible ... " what?

ELMIRA
Terrible aspect.

MICHAEL
We don't look that bad.

FRANK
What'll people think when they read that?

JOHN
They didn't print the business aspect.

FRANK
When they don't say *why* you burn someone's barn or kill their cattle it makes you like a hooligan.

THE RAILWAY TRACKS.

The field indicated in Genesis — wet, grey, the snow receding.

THE RAWLINSON HOUSE.

The house in darkness. The sound of water dripping from melting ice. Suddenly, a hideous scream.

THE RAWLINSON HOUSE. THE KITCHEN.

A luminous, wizened old face turns away, dissolving into darkness. Frank stares after it, eyes red-rimmed, stark raving mad.

Elmira descends the staircase
carrying a candle.

ELMIRA
Where's the lamp oil?

FRANK
We don't need that no more, it's a waste of money. We must not eat, we must not spend, we must not waste, we are all damned, you understand?

ELMIRA
I understand.

She goes down the back corridor.

AN UPSTAIRS BEDROOM.

Michael in bed, tossing and turning, moaning to himself. John, with a crowbar, ever so quietly pries the wainscotting away from the wall.

THE KITCHEN.

A rope is thrown over a meat hook and drawn into a knot. Frank stands on a chair, finishes the knot in the noose and throws it over his head. He picks up the bottle, takes a long drink, and totters as the bottle falls to the floor and rolls.

THE RAILWAY TRACKS.

The field referred to in Genesis. The snow has disappeared.

THE RAWLINSON BARN.

The sound of the cock-crow.

THE RAWLINSON HOUSE. THE KITCHEN.

The clock has started ticking. Frank is still standing on the chair, the noose around his neck. Michael, John, Elmer, eating. Ellen pours out a mug of tea, crosses to Frank, holds it up to him.

ELLEN
Now you going to eat your breakfast or not?

She hands him the mug of tea. He takes it.

FRANK
You think I don't got the guts, well you will see.

ELLEN
It'd take more guts to live in your case.

THE BARN. THE LOFT AND GRANARY.

A grain chute. Latimer comes up with a heavy sack of feed on his shoulder. He takes the knife to cut it and is about to dump it down the chute when he stops suddenly, hearing Isaac's voice.

ISAAC
... and they're all lookin at each other.

THE STABLE BELOW.

A stall. Elmira milking a cow. Nearby, Isaac is forking manure.

ISAAC
So what's to stop you? ... There's nothing. You see what I mean?

Elmira does not respond.

ISAAC
I always liked you, you knew that ... And you always liked me, didn't you?

ELMIRA
More or less. I guess. I have.

Isaac comes round behind her, carrying the fork.

ISAAC
I want you and me to get that money.

THE LOFT. THE GRANARY.

Latimer listening, his suspicions confirmed.

THE STABLE.

Isaac stands by Elmira. She gets up from her milking stool and turns to him.

ELMIRA
You're saying you know where it is?

Isaac puts his hand gently on her shoulder.

ISAAC
I'm saying that, yeah. Then we can go straight to the minister.

He slips his arm around her.

ISAAC
I want you to know something ... You been like a sister to me.

ELMIRA
Well then, you got to listen to me. My Granpa left me that money ... Now did he tell you where he told me?
(pause)
I'll meet you outside when I'm done milkin.

She crosses to the grain chute where it issues into a bin, picks up a bucket.

THE BARN LOFT. DAY.

Latimer listening by the chute. He sees Elmira scoop a bucket full of feed. He whispers:

LATIMER
Hey ... !

She looks up.

LATIMER
The frost's out of the ground.

ELMIRA
No! Not yet!

LATIMER
I'm going for it! It's now or never!

ELMIRA
We got to wait til they go into town.

LATIMER
They go into town twice a year! Now meet me out there.

ELMIRA
They'll see we're missing.

LATIMER
You coming with me or not?

ELMIRA
You running out on me?

LATIMER

Who's running out on who? You were just talking to him.

She looks over her shoulder.

ELMIRA

I'll explain. I can't talk now.

LATIMER

You got nothing to explain.

Latimer dumps the grain.

ELMIRA

You don't understand. Wait til noon, do you—

But the grain drowns out her words as it pours down into the bin. She peers up. He is gone.

THE DRIVE SHED.

Latimer glances over his shoulder, moves quickly into the shed, quietly pulls a shovel down from the wall.

THE BARNYARD.

Isaac and Elmira by a big dark wet manure heap, the land stretching away in drizzle and fog. Elmira produces a document.

Isaac
One day all this is going to be yours and mine.

Elmira
This here's the will Granpa left me. Now look here, it's located in the shadow cast by the second dead elm from the creek ... on November 16, at 9:30 a.m. There's his signature.

Isaac looks at it, looks dimly at Elmira. He was likely in on the killing of Hiram Bradley.

Isaac
So where's that?

Elmira
That elm that's dead by the creek. I marked the spot in November. We can go down there and dig tonight.

Isaac
Granpa told me the same.

Elmira
No he did not. He wouldn't have.

Isaac
I dug all around there.

Elmira smiles, looks him in the eye.

ELMIRA
And what you find there, Isaac?

ISAAC
Hard clay down there. You can't dig. There's nothin down there.

ELMIRA
Well I know what is.

Isaac looks at her sidelong.

ELMIRA
And it looks to me like you know what is.

ISAAC
I know nothin there.

ELMIRA
Hiram Bradley.

Isaac smiles at her.

ELMIRA
You bastard.

ISAAC
A lady don't talk like that.

ELMIRA
Come up with the money, or I go to the law ... And I mean the big law. In Toronto.

Isaac seizes her by the arm.

ISAAC
You come on with me, get in the house afore you get into trouble.

He pulls her off.

ANOTHER DREARY FIELD.

The snow has disappeared. Latimer running, breathless, half walk-ing, carrying the shovel and a length of cord. He glances over his shoulder.

THE RAILWAY TRACKS. MORNING.

Latimer walking along the ties, counting them out, carrying the shovel and a coiled cord.

LATIMER
Thirty-one ... thirty-two ... thirty-three ...

THE RAWLINSON KITCHEN. MORNING.

John, Michael and Elmer finishing their breakfast. Frank still stand-ing in the noose, Ellen clearing the table and washing up. Michael looks up suddenly ... Something is very wrong.

MICHAEL
Hell ...

JOHN
What?

The others look over at Michael.

MICHAEL
You hear something?

ELLEN
What?

MICHAEL
That ticking sound.

JOHN
(pause)
It's the clock.

MICHAEL
It just started up.

JOHN
So?

MICHAEL
I known a clock to stop, but never a one to start up like that.

Elmira comes in the door, followed by Isaac. She begins to help Ellen clear the table. Isaac sits down.

FRANK
What time does it say?

Ellen takes Frank's tea mug from him. She glances at the clock.

ELLEN
Well nigh on the hour of three less one wanting eight minutes and two.

FRANK
(pause)
What?

ELMIRA
Almost ten to two.

ELLEN
That's when it stopped in December.

FRANK
Don't matter. Just use that time now.

JOHN
What'll we do when it gets dark? Might be the wrong time.

FRANK
It's always dark, more or less.

Ellen passes Frank, belts him lightly.

ELLEN
You'd best be careful. We might need that chair and I been feeling a mite
practical lately.
(she looks around)
Where's the hired hand?

ELMIRA
He's still asleep.

THE RAILWAY TRACKS. MORNING.

Latimer kneeling between the rails on the 77th tie. He knots the cord
to one of the rails. A thick mist is developing.

THE RAWLINSON HOUSE. THE KITCHEN. MORNING.

Frank, still on the chair with the noose, staring mournfully out the
window. He frowns in perplexity, slowly turning to amazement.

FRANK
By God!

Ellen follows his gaze. She rises slowly ...

ELLEN
God almighty!

Elmer, John and Michael rise, staring, thunder-struck.

MICHAEL
The snow's gone!

FRANK
It's spring!

Isaac is in the corner, shaving. He glances at Elmira through the mirror. Elmira, washing dishes, glances back at him through the mirror.

FRANK
(hollers with joy)
Spring is nigh upon us, we've labour to commence!

MICHAEL &
JOHN
(in unison with Frank)
Spring is nigh upon us, we've labour to commence!

FRANK
(hollers)
Elmer! Get that hired man out of bed!

Elmer goes up. Elmira quickly hangs up her apron, picks up a feather duster and crosses to the corridor. Isaac follows her with his eyes. She opens a door to a downstairs bedroom.

THE UPSTAIRS CORRIDOR. MORNING.

Elmer goes down to the west bedroom, knocks. There is no response. He opens it.

THE DOWNSTAIRS BEDROOM. MORNING.

Elmira crosses, unlocks a window, yanks it open and climbs out.

THE FIELD BY THE TRACKS. MORNING.

Latimer pulls the cord seventeen feet perpendicular from the rail. With his free hand he spears the shovel into the ground, drops the cord, and begins to dig.

THE RAWLINSON HOUSE. THE KITCHEN. DAY.

Elmer runs down the stairs, crosses straight to the kitchen cupboard, opens it, picks up a shotgun.

ELMER
He's gone.

Ellen, Isaac cleaning up from shaving, John, Michael, all look up suddenly. Frank shouts from the noose.

FRANK
What do you mean, he's gone!?

The Rawlinsons explode to life, pulling on coats, tearing open drawers, pulling out revolvers, seizing a rifle from the cupboard.

FRANK
Catch him for God's sakes!

Ellen turns.

ELLEN
Careful, there!

As Frank falls, she catches him round the waist, holds him up, slackening the noose as the others head for the door.

FRANK
I didn't know you cared.

ELLEN
I'd let go if I did.
(shouts)
Michael, get back here.

Michael turns at the door.

ELLEN
Slip the rope off the hook, get him down.

MICHAEL
There isn't time, the hired man's after the money!

ELLEN
(to Michael)
Don't you see, for God's sake we're stuck here!

MICHAEL
You married him.

Michael turns to the door.

FRANK
If this goes to law, I'll do all I can to cut you out, you sonofabitch. Get me down!

Michael turns back.

MICHAEL
Since when was there law? And what the hell ever you do for me anyway, you old bastard!

ELLEN
I can't hold him up much longer!

MICHAEL
(pause; to Frank)
All right ... I want you to sing "The Farmer in the Dell, hey ho the merry-O" and then "Ba-Ba Black sheep."

Frank glares at him seething, he begins to strangle as Ellen sinks, her knees buckling.

MICHAEL
Sing it! ... Come on! In a high little girlie voice! Come on!

THE FIELD BY THE TRACKS.

Latimer digging, knee-deep; thick fog is gathering.

ANOTHER FIELD.

Frank, carrying a rifle, moves with Ellen and Michael through thickening fog. Ellen and Michael wield revolvers. Michael is shaking his head, laughing to himself.

Frank shouts across to John, Elmer and Isaac, a short distance away. Elmer has a shotgun; the other two carry revolvers.

FRANK
Fan out! I want them shot afore they're off the property. And bury 'em where they fall!

THE EDGE OF A BUSH. THICKENING FOG.

Elmira disappears into undergrowth.

ANOTHER FIELD. FOG.

Ellen, Frank and John moving quickly, scanning the country. John veers off.

THE EDGE OF THE SAME BUSH.

Isaac moving quickly, quietly with his shotgun.

DEEPER INTO THE BUSH.

Elmira stumbles through heavy underbrush.

LOW, WET LAND NEAR THE TRACKS. HEAVY FOG.

John and Michael moving quickly along the ties.

PASTURE. ELSEWHERE. HEAVY FOG.

Frank and Ellen stop, peer through the fog, change direction.

IN THE BUSH. FOG. DARK AS TWILIGHT.

Isaac reaches the spot traversed by Elmira. He sees something ahead. It is Elmira, barely visible, disappearing.

ISAAC
Elmira! You stop or I'll shoot, you hear?!

He runs, clambering through the bush and standing water, takes aim.

AHEAD THROUGH THE BUSH.

Elmira runs, clambering, stumbling through brambles. Her face and hands bloody with scratches, her dress muddy and torn. A gunshot explodes behind her, ripping off bark and whizzing in the branches by her head.

A HILLTOP IN FOG.

Frank and Ellen trudging, breathless. Hearing distant gunshots, they move off in the direction of the shots.

THE FIELD BY THE TRACKS. DENSE FOG.

Latimer is digging furiously. His shovel scrapes on wood. Breathless, he begins to clear the soil. Another distant gunshot. He looks up, straightens, wonders about Elmira. He moves to run toward the sound, looks back at the hole in indecision. He is torn, ambivalent, but finally turns back to the hole and resumes tearing away at the earth, looks up again. Elmira materializes in the fog, running, breathless, almost dropping. She stops before the hole.

ELMIRA
You could have waited.

LATIMER
It was now or never.

ELMIRA
Well they're all out after us.

He stops digging, looks up at her.

LATIMER
I just wish you'd told me, that's all.

ELMIRA
Told you what?

LATIMER
We can't argue now.

ELMIRA
Told you what?

THE TRACKS. NEAR THE WOODS. DENSE FOG.

Isaac emerges from the woods, approaches Michael near the tracks.

THE FIELD BY THE TRACKS.

Latimer and Elmira by the hole.

ELMIRA
Told you what? Go on, say it.

LATIMER
(pause)
You *know* what.

ELMIRA
(pause)
All right. How did you know?

Latimer takes hold of the trunk, deep in the hole.

LATIMER
Give me a hand with this.

They struggle to haul it out.

ELMIRA
How did you know?

LATIMER
I overheard.

They half drag the trunk out of the hole.

ELMIRA
Well so did I. I never knew neither.

They are now facing one another over the unopened trunk.

LATIMER
You never knew.

ELMIRA
He was never my type anyway. Besides he killed Hiram Bradley. I just found out.

Latimer swings the shovel, breaks open the lid, looks in, dead-pan. Elmira frowns. They are looking at a corpse, but older, more decayed this time, wearing a dark suit and hat.

LATIMER
You court this one too?

ELMIRA
That was Bill Nimrod. He sold magic lantern slides.

THE RAWLINSON HOUSE — NOW A SHADOW IN FOG.

Elmer steps up onto the veranda carrying his shotgun, goes in the kitchen door.

THE EDGE OF A FIELD. DENSE FOG.

Latimer and Elmira half running, walking,

ELMIRA
We got to get us a coach out of here or they'll run us down on the road with horses. You got cash?

They reach a road, Latimer stops.

LATIMER
God dammit, my money!

ELMIRA
What money?

LATIMER
Back in my room. I had money when I came here. I don't have anything else. Look —

ELMIRA
No! You'll be shot!

LATIMER
They all left!

ELMIRA
No!

LATIMER
Stay right here.

Elmira grabs him but he breaks from her, disappears in the fog.

THE RAWLINSON HOUSE. THE KITCHEN.

Latimer lets himself in, listens, moves across to the staircase.

THE UPSTAIRS CORRIDOR.

Latimer finds his door ajar.

THE WEST BEDROOM.

He steps in, looks around. The room is empty. He goes to the back of the door where his suit jacket hangs, goes through the pockets, finds them empty. He pulls his suitcase from under the bed, throws it down, opens it. He turns and opens the cupboard only to find Elmer discernible in the gloom, a shotgun in one hand, Latimer's wallet in the other.

ELMER
You looking for this?

LATIMER
What are you — ?

ELMER
Shouldn't have come back.

LATIMER
(*loudly, so he can hear*)
I don't know what you're talking about.

ELMER
Can't hear you. Speak up!

LATIMER
I said I don't know what you're —

ELMER
Where'd you shift the money to?

LATIMER
(*shouts*)
What money?

ELMER
Only on Saturdays and four if you're in Magog. Now tell me where you shifted the money.

LATIMER
I don't know anything about any money!

ELMER
Don't change the subject.

Elmer's thumb pulls back both hammers of the gun.

ELMER
You got one minute to tell me, then I'll blow your head off.

LATIMER
Under the 84th railroad tie from the north boundary!

ELMER
What was that?

LATIMER
(shouts)
I'll write it down!

ELMER
(shouts)
I can't read!

LATIMER
(shouts)
Get out there now while there's fog!

ELMER
Eighty-fourth what?

LATIMER
(shouts)
Railroad ... tie ... from the north boundary!

Elmer pulls a piece of cord from his pocket.

ELMER
Turn around, cross your hands behind your back.

LATIMER
Oh, God.

Latimer turns around.

THE RAWLINSON HOUSE. THE VERANDA. HEAVY FOG.

The kitchen door bursts open and Latimer emerges tied on the end of the cord which in turn is tied to Elmer's belt. With a shovel on his shoulder, Elmer pushes Latimer along at shotgun point. Not only is there fog, but it is getting darker with the afternoon. They vanish in the obscurity.

A FIELD.

Ellen, trudging along, discerns something through the fog; indeed, it is Elmer, seen from behind, carrying the shovel and shotgun. She cannot see Latimer.

ELLEN
(hollers)
Elmer's headed toward the tracks with a shovel!

ELSEWHERE. AFTERNOON, IN GATHERING GLOOM.

Isaac moving with his rifle.

ISAAC
(hollers)
Where are the tracks!?

A FIELD.

Ellen hollering.

ELLEN
Where are you?

Isaac comes up behind her.

ISAAC
Right here.

ELLEN
Oh, that's you.
(shouts)
Frank!

FRANK
(calls from somewhere nearby)
What?

ELLEN
The 4:10'll be along! Get Elmer away from the tracks. It's dangerous!

FRANK
(from somewhere)
Why?

ELLEN
He might know where the money is!

FRANK
Where are the tracks!

THE RAILWAY LINE. AFTERNOON.

The train hurtles through fog.

THE TRACKS. DARKENING .

Latimer and Elmer shrouded in fog — Latimer seated with his back
to one rail as Elmer ties the free end of the rope to it. Latimer is struggling, hollering:

LATIMER
There's a train coming!

Elmer pushes him, oblivious.

LATIMER
I said there's a train coming — the 4:10!

THE ROAD. FOG.

Elmira worried to distraction, pacing. She stops, peers through the fog.

ELSEWHERE IN THE FOG.

Frank, carrying his revolver.

FRANK
Where are the tracks!

IN THE FOG.

Michael, wandering, beginning to run.

MICHAEL
How should I know? Where are you?

SOMEWHERE BEYOND, IN THE FOG.

John, searching, breaking into a run.

JOHN
I'm right here. Hurry!

SOMEWHERE IN BETWEEN, IN OBSCURITY.

John and Michael run blindly past each other through fog.

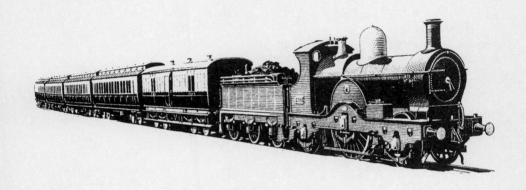

THE TRACKS. IN TWILIT FOG.

Elmer, carrying a crowbar, the shovel and shotgun, walking the ties.

ELMER
Sixty-seven ... Sixty-eight ... sixty-nine ...

A BEND IN THE TRACKS TOWARD CANAAN.

The train comes thundering around — the single eye of its lantern beaming through the fog.

IN FIELDS APPROACHING THE TRACKS. A VAST, GREY MIASMA.

The Rawlinsons are scattered, unable to see one another.

ELLEN
(hollers)
El-mer!

Isaac, elsewhere.

ISAAC
He's deaf! Where are the tracks!

Michael, lost.

MICHAEL
I'm right here!

Isaac, moving.

ISAAC
He's over there!

Frank, stumbling blindly.

FRANK
No, the tracks!

THE TRACKS. THE 84th TIE.

Elmer, using enormous strength, pries up one of the rails with the crowbar. The whistle of train blasts twice in the distance. Elmer hears nothing.

THE TRACKS. A HALF MILE AWAY.

The train bearing down through the gloom.

THE TRACKS.

Latimer bound to the rail. He scrambles in panic, straining at the cord, the steel thunder of the approaching train, as yet invisible in the fog. Latimer looks down the tracks. He can barely see the form of Elmer jimmying at the tracks, finally jacking up a tie and shifting the rail loose.

SECONDS ALONG THE TRACK.

The entire front of the demonic engine.

THE FIELDS IN MURK.

John running in fog.

JOHN
There's a train coming!

Frank
(*unseen*)
What!

John
I'm not talking to you!

THE TRACKS. THE 84th TIE.

Elmer has torn away two ties now, bent back the rail and is digging, leisurely. The roar of the train is deafening.

THE TRACKS, FURTHER ALONG.

Latimer struggles, strains, turns his face away.

THE TRACKS. THE 84th TIE.

Elmer excavates slowly in the deafening roar as the baleful light wells up in the fog.

THE TRACKS, FURTHER ALONG.

Latimer, resigned.

IN THE VICINITY OF THE TRACKS.

Frank, Ellen, Michael and John Rawlinson, all running as the ground is shaken by a terrific thundering crash and the cacophony of a wreck that seems to go on forever, followed by the explosion of the boiler.

THE TRACKS IN DEEP GLOOM.

The ghostly forms of lurching carriages, freight cars. Chaos.

THE ROAD. FOG.

Elmira, stalk still, listening to the fading of the crash. She tears off
the road into the field.

THE TRACKS. INFERNAL DUSK.

Carnage. In the midst of it, Latimer, still seated, bound to the rail,
only feet from the twisted rails where the engine plunged off. Behind
him, the toppled hulks of the wreck, a fire beginning. Smoke adding
to a vision of hell.

THE WRECK. SMOKE FOG. FIRE.

The blackened, torn and twisted body of Elmer actually moves, tries to stand, collapses. The wreckage fully in flames. Cars jack-knifed. Filthy smoke filling the air. Injured passengers screaming.

Frank, Ellen, Isaac, John and Michael drift in — dark and dreadful vultures, combing the wreckage. Isaac comes on the body of Elmer.

ISAAC
He's over here!

John and Michael join him. They drag the body away, exposing the excavation. Without a pause Isaac begins digging, while John and Michael shift the splinterd ties and rails.

THE OTHER SIDE OF THE TOPPLED LOCOMOTIVE.

Latimer, stunned and blackened. He looks up. Out of the fog materializes a tramp, scarcely human: a frightful, weatherbeaten scarecrow in rags. He carries a small sack. But the face that emerges is that of Granpa. Latimer stares at him emptily.

GRANPA
This has happened before, it will happen again.

He kneels, pulls out a jack-knife and frees Latimer from the tracks.

GRANPA
Over and over.

Latimer stumbles, staggers.

LATIMER
(groggily)
Who are you?

GRANPA
Come on now, quick, get a move on.

Granpa tugs him by the sleeve. They disappear in fog.

A WRECKED PASSENGER CARRIAGE.

Ellen, blackened with soot, tears out wood siding as a dead passenger rolls out. Frank opens suitcases nearby.

ELLEN
(shouts)
I always said to Elmer, share and share alike, but he never listened.

FRANK
He was deaf!

THE TRACKS. A DISTANCE AHEAD.

Elmira makes her way along through the fog. She sees someone approaching her.

ELMIRA
Oh, Latimer! Thank heavens to God!

Running, she collides, embracing him. But it is Granpa. She shrieks in horror. Then Latimer materializes. Elmira recognizes the old man.

ELMIRA
(beside herself)
Granpa!

GRANPA
(smiles)
You're lookin good.

ELMIRA
(to Latimer)
It's my Granpa!
(in tears, to Granpa)
What happened!

GRANPA
The rope broke!

ELMIRA
I know, but —

GRANPA
There was a landslide in
the cemetery.

ELMIRA
This is the hired hand,
Latimer Davenport.

GRANPA
I know who you are.
(smiles)
I sold your mother there
some trash in the win-
tertime.

ELMIRA
How did you — ?

GRANPA
Don't worry about the money.

ELMIRA
I'm not worried about the money.

LATIMER
Elmira — hold on, wait —

Grandpa presses some cash into Elmira's hand.

143

GRANPA

The money's still where I shifted it to. But this should get you out of here cause you'd better get off now with your hides.

He turns to leave.

GRANPA

I ain't gone yet.

But before he disappears he stops and turns back to Elmira.

GRANPA

But when I am, you're my only blood descendant, my sole inheritor.

Latimer pulls Elmira, and they disappear into the fog.

THE TRAIN WRECK.

The Rawlinsons, blackened with soot, foraging. Frank drags out a bloody passenger, tries to open the man's jacket. He turns to a figure in the foggy darkness.

FRANK

Just grab a-hold, give me a hand there, will you?

He finds himself face to face with his father, screams in horror.

THE RAWLINSON HOUSE. THE KITCHEN. DUSK.

The room is barely lit. Elmer's mangled body lies on the table, surrounded with dinner services, jewellery, clothing, parasols, suitcases, a couple of paintings, some bronzes. Frank, Ellen, Isaac, John and Michael blackened with soot, standing around, their division of the booty brought to a halt. They are facing Granpa, who has just come in the door. He addresses Frank.

GRANPA
Barn roof's in bad repair. Why ain't you fixed it?
(to Ellen)
Make up that west bedroom ... I reckon I'm going to die again ...

He breaks out into a chuckling, braying laugh — the Rawlinsons, distraught.

THE RAILWAY. BRIGHT, OPEN COUNTRYSIDE.

The Maskinonge Central sails through farm land.

A PASSENGER CARRIAGE.

Latimer, dressed in his city clothes. Elmira asleep with her head on his shoulder.

COUNTRYSIDE

The train disappears round a bend, and passes, blasting its whistle through the beaten pastures of the Rawlinson property and its decrepit homestead — and the window of the west bedroom.

John Reeves

Hugh Graham